Walks
East Cambr

Cambridge Group of
The Ramblers' Association

Walks in East Cambridgeshire

Published by the
Cambridge Group of The Ramblers' Association
with grant aid and support from Cambridgeshire County
Council and the Countryside Commission

Acknowledgements

The following helped in the publication of this booklet:
Nigel C Balchin – editing and typesetting
Alistair A Cook, Mary Davidson, David Ellis, Jenny Ellis,
David Harrison, John Hunter, Lyn Jenkins, Vic Jenkins,
Janet Moreton, Roger Moreton – maps, Christine Pizey,
Margaret Rishbeth, David Shepherd, Jill Tuffnell,
Pauline Wynn, Ron Wilbraham – cover illustrations
Cambridgeshire County Council – Rural Management Group
Suffolk County Council
Soham Footpath Society – Chris Turnbull

The maps in the booklet are based upon the Ordnance Survey
Landranger map Sheets 143 (1992) and 154 (1991), with the
permission of the Controller of Her Majesty's Stationery Office
© Crown copyright

First published 1992, reprinted 1996

ISBN 0 9522518 0 9

PLEASE NOTE: Since the first printing, many trunk roads in
the area have been renumbered.

Ramblers' Association National Office
  1-5 Wandsworth Road
  London SW8 2XX

Local contact addresses at time of printing:
  John Capes, 30 Queensway, Sawston, Cambridge CB2 4DJ
  R & J Moreton, 23 Emery Street, Cambridge CB1 2AX
  Jill Tuffnell, 62 Beche Road, Cambridge CB5 8HU

Local government department responsible for footpath maintenance:
Rural Management Team, Property Department,
Cambridgeshire County Council,
Shire Hall, Cambridge CB3 0AP

Introduction

Like the Cambridge Group's earlier 'Walks in South Cambridgeshire', this book is based broadly on a local government district. While most of the walks are circular, starting and finishing in East Cambridgeshire, there are two linear walks, one starting in East Cambridgeshire, the other starting and finishing in Suffolk, but crossing East Cambridgeshire on the way.

East Cambridgeshire District extends from Burrough Green and Kirtling, south of Newmarket, northwards to Soham, Ely and Littleport, and westwards to Haddenham and Mepal; but a large bite taken out of its western boundary places Exning and Newmarket in Suffolk. It thus includes a wide variety of landscapes, with high chalklands in the south giving way to peat fens in the north and west, and to poorer and lighter soils in the east where the chalk is overlaid by blown sand instead of glacial boulder-clay on the borders of the Breckland. Also included is the extensive clay 'Isle of Ely' in the Fens, once the centre of its own community.

The chalky boulder-clay country has heavy soils, mostly given over to cereal farming, with patches of oilseed rape – although the brilliant yellow flowers of the latter are now slowly giving way to linseed, or flax, also grown for oil, but much less strident in its delicate blue appearance and smell.The soil lightens progressively to the north and east, and near Kirtling and Dullingham are large areas of established woodland, well-populated with pheasants and deer.

Towards Newmarket the arable land gives way to extensive stud farms, with miles of wooden railings and little wooden stables dotted about the grassland, reminiscent of the stone barns of Swaledale in Yorkshire. A word of warning – racehorses are highly strung beasts, which should be treated with caution, as noted under 'Safety and comfort' below. Chalkland flowers bloom on ditch-banks and road verges. Part of the Devils Dyke, a massive linear earthwork from the Dark Ages, is now managed by the Cambridgeshire and Bedfordshire Wildlife Trust and the Cambridgeshire County Council as a nature reserve free from weedkillers and intensive cultivation, with knapweed, scabious, toadflax, the sinister parasitic tall broomscape, and colonies of the scarce bloody cranesbill.

To the west of Newmarket, the fen-edge villages and former inland ports of Bottisham, the Swaffhams, Reach, Burwell, Wicken and Soham each have a once-navigable 'lode' connecting to the Cam or Great Ouse rivers. North and west are the flat Fens, where walking is largely restricted to the banks of rivers and intersecting dykes or drains, and to the fen droves, many of which are attractive 'green lanes', sometimes open, sometimes hedged, and often astonishingly wide. Observant map-readers will note that few of these are marked as public rights of way on any but the most recent Ordnance Survey maps – during the 1950s the then Isle of Ely county was dilatory in registering them, and it took the 1981 Wildlife and Countryside Act to induce their successors to complete the task. The flatness of the prospect is relieved by the banks of of rivers raised above ground level on their way to the sea. These include the massive banks of the Hundred Foot Drain, built in the 17th century to carry water from the Great Ouse to the sea at Kings Lynn, and currently being strengthened by the National Rivers Authority. Look out for the pumping engines built to raise water from the fen below, of which Stretham Old Engine (walk 11) is a fascinating steam-driven survivor. Ely Cathedral stands high on its 'island', an enduring monument to the faith of its builders, sighted during nearly every walk in this booklet.

Farming in the Fens is again intensive and arable, but with a much wider variety of crops than on the heavy boulder-clay soil; three-quarters of Britain's root crops are grown in East Anglia. Interesting plant and bird life, like some of the walking, is concentrated beside the waterways, with an exuberance of high-summer weeds – a joy to see, but they can be difficult to walk through! Look out for the gorgeous purple loosestrife, and the brown-headed ram-rods of reed mace – commonly but incorrectly called bulrushes. Wicken Fen, a survivor of the original Fen landscape, owned by the National Trust, is open to the public for a small charge. Walks 15 and 20 together provide an almost complete circuit on public paths on the banks of its boundary dykes. This viewpoint shows the shrinkage of the drained peat in the surrounding land, due to oxidation, which was measured as 'the height of a man in the life of a man'; the little wooden windmill in the Fen now pumps water in to prevent its peat drying out.

In contrast to Wicken Fen, Chippenham Fen just north of Newmarket is a pocket of low-lying marshland through which passes a tributary of the River Snail. It is a National Nature Reserve, with a variety of orchids and wetland plants; although not generally open to the public, it can be seen from the public footpath – walk 17.

South of the Fens, around Haddenham and Wilburton, the peat soil is replaced by older beds of clay, with market gardens and plum and apple orchards. To the east the transition to the Breckland is marked by the appearance of rows of old, misshapen Scots pines, remnants of earlier shelter-belts, a very characteristic feature of the West Suffolk landscape. The sluggish Cam and Great Ouse are replaced by livelier chalk streams such as the Rivers Lark and Snail, running clear over stony beds.

The walks in this book have been chosen to give a good spread over the whole area, so far as the existing public path network will allow. Some of the routes connect with those in the South Cambridgeshire volume, and longer walks can be made on three long-distance routes. The Icknield Way Recreational Route from Ivinghoe Beacon, Buckinghamshire, to Knettishall Heath, Suffolk, sponsored by the Countryside Commission, crosses the area from Burrough Green to Cheveley; it should be fully waymarked. The other two were devised by the Ramblers' Association; the Hereward Way from Stamford, Lincolnshire, to Knettishall Heath, Suffolk, crosses from Little Downham to Prickwillow. The Stour Valley Walk follows the river valley from near Newmarket to the sea at Shotley Gate, near Ipswich, Suffolk, past Kirtling and Great Bradley. For further information, see 'Other published walks' on page 12.

Local terms

Drove   Unsurfaced roadway used by pedestrians and cattle

Dyke   Drainage channel
         or earth bank for flood control
         or bank and ditch for defence

Lode   Water-filled channel between raised banks, for
         navigation and drainage

Hoggin   Track surface of compacted stone, usually
         orange-coloured

Public paths

The various paths – footpaths, bridleways and byways – used on the walks in this book are nearly all public rights of way, but their condition may vary; the exceptions are 'permitted paths' used with the landowner's permission, and usually in good condition.

Where paths cross farmland, the farmer must not obstruct them with fences, hedges or crops. In general, paths along field boundaries may not be ploughed, and must be at least 1.5 metres wide for footpaths, or 3 metres for bridleways. Paths across fields may be ploughed, but must be restored to be visible and convenient for walking within two weeks, and kept clear of crops for a width of 1 metre. These duties are laid down in the Rights of Way Act, 1990. Overgrown paths need to be cleared by the County Council.

Although all the walks have been carefully checked during 1992, and the Rural Management department of the Cambridgeshire County Council ensured that the paths were clear and well-signposted, problems inevitably arise from time to time; for example, official path diversions and other changes may necessitate slight alterations in the route.

If you are unfortunate enough to encounter difficulties, please inform the local Footpath Secretary of the Ramblers' Association; see the reverse of the title page. If you would like to help the Rambler's Association to improve footpaths, why not join? You could also take an active part in waymarking and path clearance.

Circular and Linear Walks

Most of the walks described in this booklet are 'circular walks', that is, you walk round a circuit, returning to your starting point. Walks 29 and 30 are linear, needing advance planning of your return journey; they are more easily followed using public transport from Cambridge and back.

Route indication

Each walk description has a map, on which the route has been picked out with a thick line ━━━ shown interrupted ━ ━ ━ where the route follows a road. Alternative or short-cut routes are shown with shorter dashes ▪▪▪▪▪.

Waymarks

Small arrows of various colours on special posts or on stiles, or painted on walls, indicate routes which may be used by walkers and others. The Countryside Commission code is:

Yellow – public footpath
Blue – public bridleway
Red – public byway, may be used by vehicles
White – permitted route, the landowner allows the public to
         walk

Public transport

Rail – Ely has good services from Cambridge, London, Peterborough and Kings Lynn. Newmarket is an unmanned station on the Bury St. Edmunds – Cambridge line.

Bus – Ely and Newmarket have services from Cambridge and other large centres, and services to some nearby villages. A Cambridgeshire County Council leaflet published in 1992 listed the routes available.

Up-to-date information should be requested from the operators; telephone numbers in summer 1992 were:
British Rail   Cambridge (0223) 311999
Cambus   Cambridge (0223) 423554

Car parking

Please observe the restrictions on location and duration of parking, and charges; this applies mainly in the City of Ely, and in Newmarket. Suggested car parks are:
Ely – Barton Road
Newmarket – Rookery shopping centre

In rural areas, be careful not to obscure the view of other road users, and do not obstruct farm and field entrances.

Refreshments

Ely and Newmarket have many public houses, cafes and restaurants. Where appropriate, facilities in other places, or the lack of them, are noted.

Abbreviations

PH   Public House
N   north   E   east   S   south   W   west

Maps

Our aim has been to make it possible to follow the routes with the aid of this booklet alone, but a map will help, enabling the location of features of interest, the choice of alternative routes to increase or decrease the distance to be covered, or just to get acquainted with the use of a map.

For each walk, we give the sheet numbers of appropriate Ordnance Survey maps from the Landranger 1:50000 and Pathfinder 1:25000 series as listed below; numbers in brackets, as (941), mean that only a short length of the route falls on that sheet. The Landranger maps are almost essential for finding the more isolated starting points.

Landranger 1:50000 (mauve covers)
143   Ely & Wisbech
154   Cambridge, Newmarket & surrounding area

Pathfinder 1:25000 (green covers)
941   *TL48/58*   Ely (North) & Littleport
961   *TL47/57*   Ely (South), Haddenham & Soham
962   *TL67/77*   Mildenhall & Fordham
982   *TL46/56*   Cambridge (North) & Burwell
983   *TL66/76*   Newmarket
1005   *TL65/75*   Dullingham & Chedburgh
1028   *TL64/74*   Haverhill & Clare

The maps in the booklet are based upon the Ordnance Survey Landranger map Sheets 143 (1992) and 154 (1991), with the permission of the Controller of Her Majesty's Stationery Office © Crown copyright. They are generally to the same 1:50000 scale, except for three walks further reduced in size. Each is oriented with N to the top of the page. Letters like **H** in bold indicate points on the walk which are marked on the map. Other paths not on the route are shown as dotted lines.

National grid references are given in square brackets, for example [523781] – the letters 'TL' precede the 6 figures given here for the full reference. The point can be located on an Ordnance Survey map by looking for the first two digits, 52 in the example above, along the lower edge, and the fourth and fifth digits, 78, up the side; lines from these points meet at the bottom left-hand corner of the grid square, as shown in the diagram. Where Landranger sheets 143 and 154 are both listed, the second pair of numbers is 74 or more for sheet 143.

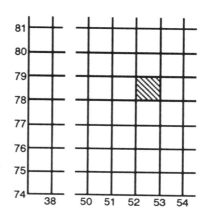

The grid numbers are reproduced in the maps in the booklet, but the Ordnance Survey does not guarantee their accuracy.

Please note that the wire binding of this booklet may affect compass readings.

Scale for route maps in this book, except where marked

Miles

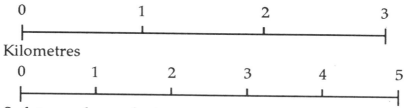

Kilometres

Safety and comfort

Footbridges may be slippery and/or narrow.

Please take care when crossing roads and especially railways.

Make sure that you are visible on roads – wear bright clothing, and carry a light at dusk or in misty weather.

Racehorses should be treated with caution; generally public paths are fenced off from the grazing land, but quiet behaviour is advised, especially with mares and foals.

Suitable footwear is advisable to cope with muddy paths in winter.

Nettles and thistles grow in profusion on many paths – stout long trousers are recommended.

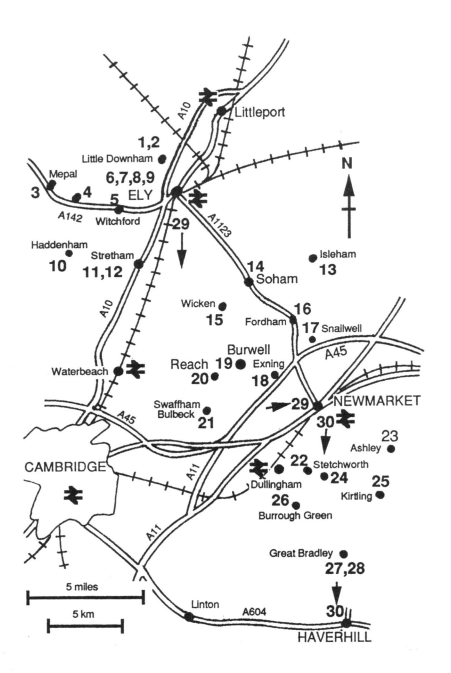

Walks

Location map on opposite page

Other published walks

These are available at Tourist Information Centres, and at some bookshops in the area.

CCC   Published by/in association with Cambridgeshire County Council

RA   Published by the Ramblers Association

O   Out-of-print, but some outlets may have a few copies

*   indicate an outline of route, without a detailed description

* Enjoying the Cambridgeshire countryside   CCC
     (a general leaflet on where to go and what to see)

Leaflet series   CCC
     Ely Nature Trail 6
     Ely Easy Access trail
     Cawdle Fen
     Fordham – Isleham railway line
     Wicken Walks
     Bishops Way
     Mepal
     Devils Dyke
     Quy Fen
     Hereward Way
     Beating the Bounds – rights of way in various parishes

Wicken Fen leaflet   National Trust

Hereward Way   RA Peterborough Group

Walks in South Cambridgeshire   RA Cambridge Group

Walks around Cambridge   RA Cambridge Group   O
     including Little Thetford – Ely

More walks around Cambridge   RA Cambridge Group   O
     including Ely – Prickwillow,
     Swaffham Prior – Prickwillow

The Icknield Way Path   Icknield Way Association

* The Cambridgeshire Fens   BBC Radio Cambridgeshire

1   Little Downham – shorter

3 miles / 5 kilometres

Start: Little Downham, Main Street **A** [527842]
Maps: Landranger 143; Pathfinder 941
Transport: Bus – from Ely
Refreshments: Little Downham – PH, shops

Points of interest:
See Walk 2

From Main Street **A**, go N down School Lane by the side of the village hall. Turn right just before the recreation ground and follow the field path to the road. Turn right, cross the road and then turn almost immediately left into California Road. Just before the sewage works, take Beild Drove **B**, the second drove on your left. Continue walking E.

At the next junction, by some rusty sheds, keep straight on. You are now walking along Coffue Drove. The track swings right and when you come to an earth bridge over a dyke, cross it. You should still have a ditch on your right. The track now swings round further to the right. It is now called Marshal Drove; follow it W as far as the Ely/Little Downham road **C**. At the junction turn left, then cross the road and turn right down Little Street. This leads to a field edge path which you should take as far as a wide cross track by a bungalow. Turn right, keeping a ditch on your right, and follow the track back into the village. Go straight over at the first cross-roads and then turn right when you meet Main Street again.

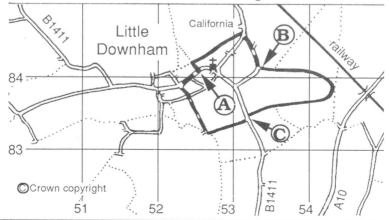

©Crown copyright

2   Little Downham – longer

7 miles / 11 kilometres

Start: Little Downham, Canon Street **A** [527839]
Maps: Landranger 143; Pathfinder 941
Transport: Bus – from Ely and Cambridge
Refreshments: Little Downham – Plough PH, Anchor PH
                       Shops and village stores

Points of interest:
Little Downham church
Downham, or Duneham, means 'home of the dunes'.
The   village was built on a ridge of sand and gravel –
hence   the name. There is evidence of vineyards and a
fruit   garden along the present-day Canon Street as
early as   1286. The current Village Centre was
previously the   guildhall of a wealthy settlement.
The area of Little Downham was the garden of the
    monastery of Ely, providing produce for the Bishop's
    table. Also in the village is the Bishop's Palace, the
    summer residence of the Bishops of Ely for more than
    500 years.

Start from Canon Street **A**, and walk W along it, passing
Bishops Way signs, following the roadway straight ahead,
swinging to the right before forming a junction with the
B1411. Turn left – unless you want early refreshments at The
Plough PH opposite! At the junction with the Pymore road turn
right. Follow the road as it swings first left – and then, just as
it turns right by Guildacre Farm, take a grassy track on your
left, just in front of some cottages. This is Land Floods Drove.
On the Pathfinder map this track is mistakenly shown as a
classified road! After half a mile the track turns sharp right,
then left, before it meets a metalled road **B**. At the road turn
left. Follow the road as it swings to the right. At the next
junction, just past Hythe Farm, turn left and back onto the
Little Downham – Coveney road. Now look out for Redcaps
Lane on your right – and turn into it.

After 350 yards the Lane meets a track by Foxey Farm barn.
Turn left. The route now follows a pleasant grassy track for
nearly three-quarters of a mile. When it swings right you must
take the footpath straight ahead – over a footbridge and then a
stile. You pass pasture for grazing horses – seemingly one of
the main features of Little Downham agriculture.

Crossing a road leading down from the village you rejoin a byway, Clayway Lane. After 200 yards, ignore the footpath on the left; keep on the track where it swings right, and follow it for 100 yards past a couple of barns, before turning left onto an earthen track. This soon swings to the right, regaining the original line of your route.

After a further 300 yards you pass a new bungalow on your right. Keep on the track as it gently veers to the right, going S – avoiding a footpath signed to the left. 400 yards further on you come to a byway sign – a red arrow on a white background – pointing along a grassy track to your left. Take this Fox's Drove, leading directly to the B1411 road.

When you get to the road **C**, cross it, picking up the Byway signposted opposite. This is called The Balk on the Pathfinder map. After 500 yards there is a track, Pithouse Drove, to the left, which you should turn down. A further 400 yards on this track in turn meets a T-junction – and here your route goes to the right, along a track called first Marshal Drove and then Coffue Drove. This grassy track first runs W/E, then swings N before coming right back on itself, following an E/W route. By Beild Drove Farm a track joins from the right, and 200 yards further on you are back on a metalled road near the sewage works!

Turn left and walk back down to the B1411 once more, passing a disused windmill on your left. At the main road turn right, and after about 250 yards Canon Street is again on your left. Or continue along the main road to look at more of the village.

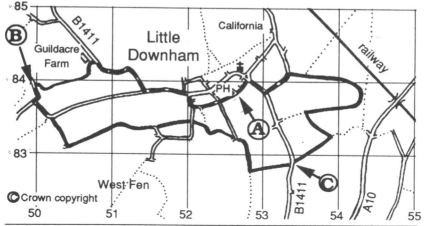

3 Mepal circular

3.5 miles / 5.5 kilometres

Start: Mepal Bridge – Three Pickerels PH **A** [441813]

Maps: Landranger 143; Pathfinder 941

Transport: Bus – from Ely

Refreshments: Mepal Bridge – Three Pickerels PH
Mepal – shop/PO

Points of interest:

Ouse Washes, internationally important nature reserve
Fortrey Hall, home of one of the Fenland Adventurers
Traces of medieval village
Former Ferryman's House
Churchyard with surviving elms
Widden's Hill, White Hill, associated with witches

Opposite the pub **A** take the footpath on the E bank of the New Bedford River. After about 500 yards there is a waymark sign pointing down a track to your right. If you only want a very short stroll this gives access to The Rushway, a pleasant path leading back into Mepal. For the longer walk described here keep straight on along the river bank. You will have to come off the bank onto a track running alongside to avoid barbed wire on a fence – but otherwise keep alongside the watercourse until you come to a small group of buildings at Witcham Gravel **B**. You have now walked about one and a quarter miles. Turn right along a track just in front of the buildings, crossing a fence next to a gate. The track soon leads you onto Gravel Drove, a tarmac roadway. Turn right. After about half a mile you come to a track running at right angles across the road, on the N bank of a watercourse, Catchwater Drain. Turn right onto the track **C**.

This path can be very muddy at the start, but conditions eventually improve. The track follows the watercourse, first W and then swinging to the N. Look out for a waymark post and bridge on your left across the Drain. Cross the bridge. On the far side take a path through open fields running in line with the bridge – W. First you cross The Rushway track, stepping over a stile on your left. You soon cross a new hoggin track, with another stile to go over. This brings you into the last field to be crossed before joining New Road in Mepal.

Walk down the road, turning left into High Street and then right into Laurel Close (shop and post office). Alternatively, look out for a footpath crossing a field to view the last remaining signs of the medieval village – on the left of the footpath. This is reached by crossing the road leading to Mepal Bridge, and emerges onto the footpath by Mepal church, where you should turn right.

When you come to a T-junction turn right and cross over, looking out for River Close and a public footpath sign to Mepal Church. Follow this path down past the church. It swings round to the river and brings you back to the Three Pickerels pub **A**.

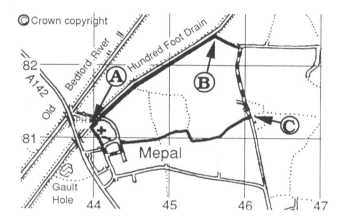

4   Witcham – Wardy Hill circular

4 miles / 6.5 kilometres

Start: Witcham, Silver Street A [463799]
Maps: Landranger 143; Pathfinder 941
Transport: Bus – from Ely
Refreshments: Witcham, White Horse Inn (PH)
Points of interest:
    Church, Witcham Hall, many other fine old buildings

From Silver Street **A** retrace your steps back to the Mepal
Road which runs N/S through the village. Take High Street
opposite (running due E). Pass the Hall and church on your
left. As you come to the T-junction with Headleys Lane, turn
left. 120 yards further on you meet Back Lane. Turn right. The
first 400 yards can be muddy; when you get to a junction of
tracks, keep right; the path becomes grassy in a pleasant
green lane which passes between mature hedges and trees.

The track turns sharp left and after 300 yards you meet a
well-used track crossing your path W/E. Turn right. In a
further 600 yards you meet a road – Long Causeway – leading
to Coveney **B**. Turn left. After half a mile the road swings first
left and then right, just past Wolvey Holes Farm. Leave the
road at this point, turning left, and keep the farm buildings on
your left. A grassy track passes between high hedges for about
30 yards, then the route opens out. Keep a hedge on your
right and an open field on your left. The track is called
Grudges Bank on the Pathfinder map. After about 300 yards it
again meets a road – this time Short Causeway. Turn left onto
the road.

You are now walking towards the settlement of Wardy Hill.
After 600 yards the road swings right **C**, but take the track –
Hale Fen Lane – which swings left, keeping a hedge on your
right. Another 600 yards on you meet a track on your left,
which you turn down. The next quarter of a mile can be very
muddy! When you meet a track crossing your path at right
angles go straight over. You are now on Wardy Hill Road, a
very broad grassy ride which runs between low hedges.

The going is fine until you come to Ivy House Farm, where it can once again become muddy. 150 yards past the farm you again meet Back Lane. Turn right and almost immediately turn left, down a path with trees on the right hand side and fencing on the left. This path takes you down by the side of the church, back to High Street. Turn right and you are once again by the recreation ground and near your start.

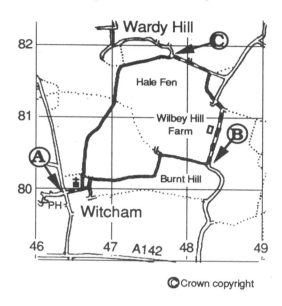

©Crown copyright

5   Witchford circular

4 miles / 6.5 kilometres

Start: Witchford church **A** [504778]

Maps: Landranger 143; Pathfinder 961, (941)

Transport: Bus – from Cambridge and Ely

Refreshments: Witchford – Shoulder of Mutton PH
                                     village store

From the church **A** walk E along the road. Near the end of the village you will see Grunty Fen Road on your right, but turn left down a track just beyond it, called Broadway. Just after an electricity sub-station on your left the tarmac ends and the track continues as grass. Keep along it, with a water course, Grunty Fen Drain, on your right. After 300 yards you pass a kissing gate on your right giving access to open land, but you veer to the left as the track you are following turns away from the Drain, keeping between high hedges. You can see the buildings of Witchford Village College across the field to your left.

The track approaches the Witchford bypass. When you get to the wooden fencing, don't go through it as if to cross the road but instead turn left. The path now swings away from the road again. In about 250 yards you come to a tarmac drive leading to the Village College. Turn right, and after a further 20 yards turn sharp right again. This track again leads back to the bypass **B**, and this time you do go across onto a wide grassy track opposite, on the right of a watercourse – Catchwater Drain. Follow this track for almost a mile.

The first buildings you pass are Ridgeway Farm, soon followed by Common Farm. Continue past the broad grassy track on your left opposite Common Farm for 150 yards, until the track turns sharp left. Follow it, with a ditch on your left, for a further half mile. When you meet a broad track running at right angles **C** turn left along it. You will have a high hedge on your left and an open field on your right – Old Fen Baulk Road on the Pathfinder map.

The track rises gradually to the high point of the walk – 16 metres above sea-level! After 600 yards, with the bypass once more in view, the track swings sharp left – Granny's End Road – then swings slightly to the right and down to the bypass. Cross the road again, going up the steps and over the stile opposite. A track takes you back to the main village road. Cross it, again taking the track immediately opposite – New Road **D**.

Haddenham lies to the SW, with a mast and water tower visible on the skyline. Follow the track due S for about three-quarters of a mile, passing an orchard on your left. You meet and cross Grunty Fen Catchwater by a clump of trees. Turn left onto the track which runs along the S bank of the watercourse. Follow this track for nearly a mile, past the landfill tip on your right, as far as Grunty Fen Road. Turn left and walk back along the road into the village – about 400 yards – until you again meet the main street. The pub is about 300 yards further on your left!

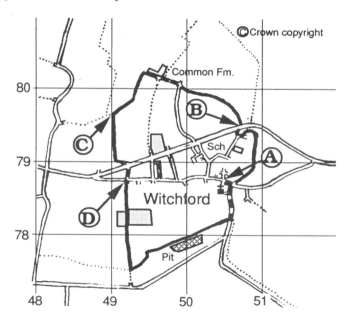

6 Ely – Littleport circular

12.5 miles / 20 kilometres

Start: Ely, Cathedral Green **A** [540803]
Maps: Landranger 143; Pathfinder 941
Transport: Rail – good connections to both Ely and
                 Littleport – this walk can be adapted to
                 two linear walks of around 7 miles each
                 by using the train between Littleport
                 and Ely – it might be worth reversing
                 the direction if there is a strong SW
                 headwind

Refreshments: Ely and Littleport – PH and cafes

Make your way to the Cathedral Green **A** and the church with
a spire opposite the Old Fire Engine House restaurant and art
gallery. Go W onto the Cambridge Road. Cross it and go into
Downham Road opposite. Keep to the left fork at the junction
80 yards on, and follow the road for the next half a mile, until
you come to the Ely bypass. Cross the bypass and go down
the road opposite. After 100 yards turn off right, along a lane
marked Public Byway. There is a sign alongside for the
Bishops Way, which we will follow towards Little Downham,
and again on our return into Ely.

This track is called Hurst Lane and passes the farm of the
same name. The tarmac surface soon turns to grass and
earth. Make sure you keep a ditch on your right. Little
Downham village can be seen clearly ahead. After about a mile
and a quarter you will see a dilapidated shed in a field on your
left. Very soon after you should find a waymark post pointing
out a byway on your right. Turn right into Fox's Drove and
continue up to the road **B**. Cross the road, turn left and then
almost immediately right, turning down another public byway,
called The Balk on the Pathfinder map.

The track can at first be muddy but conditions should
improve after a while. After 500 yards you come to a junction,
but keep on the right hand pathway, with a ditch on your
right. After 200 yards the track swings left then right. You are
again approaching the Ely bypass – but before you reach it
take a distinct vehicle track swinging left – Coffue Drove –
which runs due N for about 2.5 miles in all, but we will cut off
right to Littleport part way along it.

After 600 yards cross a watercourse – ignore the track turning off to the right just before it. 200 yards further on you come to the first of several railway crossings, here by a tunnel under the line. Keep on the track beyond for over half a mile. Just after you pass a broken down brick barn, complete with rusting van and machinery, look out for a farm track on the right. Take it. Within 250 yards you cross a wide waterway. Keep to the track, which turns first left, then right again. A further 400 yards on you pass farm buildings on your right, just before you meet Woodfen Road **C**; turn left onto it.

The Littleport bypass has turned this road into a cul-de-sac and it provides a pleasant walk into Littleport itself. Continue along it, ignoring the first road on your right which leads directly to the bypass. Further on your route swings gently right. When you meet the bypass, cross it, picking up Woodfen Road again behind the embankment ahead. It is a further half a mile to the outskirts of the village. You enter alongside the school playing fields.

Littleport

When you come to a road junction turn right into Parsons Lane – which takes you past the entrance to the school. The village centre is just over half a mile further on. By the church you proceed into Church Lane. At the traffic lights cross straight over – although as you have now passed the half way point you might like a refreshment stop at The Crown pub by the crossroads.

You are first in Main Street, then Victoria Street. A further half a mile on you cross the Kings Lynn railway line and then pass the Black Horse pub, just by the Great Ouse. Here you have a choice of routes back to Ely. If you cross the river and take the footpath on the E bank you have to keep to the riverside for 3.5 miles, where you can cross back at Queen Adelaide. If you want to return to Ely by train, take the footpath on your left to the station.

The route selected here is to stick to the W bank; so before you cross the river bridge, turn right, taking a track between houses and the actual bank. You can see Ely Cathedral clearly to your right as you walk S along the bank top. After almost two miles you cross a tributary watercourse on your right. Go through the metal gate and return to the flood bank. After half a mile prepare to turn away from the river, opposite Clayway Farm on the left bank of the Cam **D**.

You cross a wooden bridge and then cross a stile over the railway fence. Cross the line, taking extra care because of the very fast trains, to a stile opposite, which takes you to a footpath with a ditch on the right. You can see the buildings called Kettlesworth on the map straight ahead. Make for them. When you reach a wide track, just by the buildings, turn left; you are now back on the Bishops Way. After 600 yards you cross another railway line. Keep to Clayway Drove as you walk back into Ely.

Ely

When you meet the Prickwillow Road, cross over and keep to the footpath on the left. In about 500 yards you pass the Sailing Club building on your left. Turn into the drive, but turn immediately right and over a bridge onto Ely Common. You can now walk through the Common, keeping in touch with the roadway on your right. When you come to a driveway across your path, go over and through a kissing gate opposite. Continue through the Common to a second kissing gate, returning to the road. Turn left. After a quarter of a mile follow the Bishops Way sign pointing down Brays Lane on your left – it brings you back into the Market Place. To return to your start turn right and walk back to the cathedral.

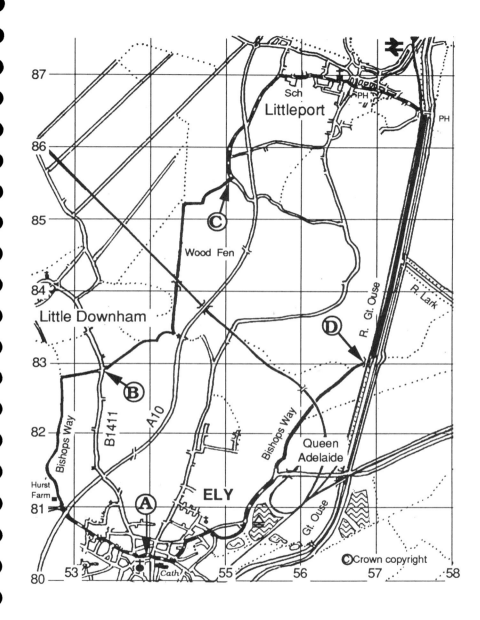

7   Ely – Prickwillow circular

9.5 miles / 15 kilometres

Start: Ely, Barton Square **A** [540800]

Maps: Landranger 143; Pathfinder 941, (961)

Refreshments: Prickwillow – The Pottery
                       Queen Adelaide – **none**

Points of interest:
     Ely Cathedral and historic buildings
     Prickwillow Pottery and Pumping Museum
     Birds on Rivers Lark and Great Ouse, and Roswell Pits
     Train spotting, especially in Queen Adelaide

Ely

From Barton Square **A** go through the archway in the monastic building – Porta – and follow the path straight on through the park. At Broad Street turn left and cross over into the first road on the right – Ship Lane. Follow the pedestrian path past The Maltings on your right. At the river turn left and follow the towpath to the bridge, but do not cross it. On the left of the bridge the path continues to Willow Walk, a grassed area.

Go under the rail bridge **B** and follow the raised bank towards buildings in the distance. Go over the stile, turn left and then right into the road. Go through the kissing gate over Cuckoo Bridge and take the path through the trees towards the river. Cross the iron bridge **C** and turn right along the road. After 150 yards, take the first track on the left, signposted Hereward Way, and follow it NE for about 2 miles to Prickwillow village.

Prickwillow

Cross the grassed area ahead – do not turn right into Putney Hill Road – to the junction of the Ely – Prickwillow road, then turn right towards the river. The Pottery and Pumping Museum are here.

Do not cross the river bridge **D**, but turn left – NW – onto the path on the W side of the River Lark. Under the rail bridge, follow the path until you reach the first turning, Second Drove **E** [593833]. Turn left onto it and walk W until you reach Branch Bank Road **F**. Cross the road and turn left on top of the embankment of the River Great Ouse towards Queen Adelaide village.

At the road bridge, cross into the village, and go over one level crossing. Immediately after – **G** – take the track on the left beside the railway. Just past the gardens go right and cross the railway – with extreme caution, blind corner – and cross the meadows diagonally to the W towards another stile at a railway track **H** – caution again. Follow the track alongside the lake to the sailing club; turn left, over a sleeper bridge onto the commons, and follow the path.

Ely

Turn left into Lisle Lane, and take the first footpath on the right behind bungalows and sheltered housing to Vineyards Road. Continue W on the road to the Market Place, and cross it diagonally into the High Street. A little way along, go through Sacrist Gate, an archway in a wall on the left, and follow the path to the left behind the Cathedral. On reaching the road follow it and go through another archway, the Porta, into Barton Square **A**.

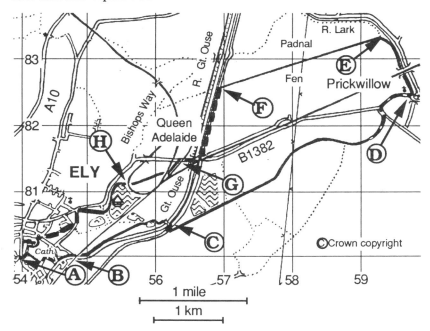

8   Ely – Queen Adelaide circular

5.5 miles / 9 kilometres

Start: Ely, Barton Square **A** [540800]
Maps: Landranger 143; Pathfinder 941
Refreshments: Ely – PH, cafes
                     Queen Adelaide – **none**

Points of interest:
        Train spotting
        Ely Cathedral
        Roswell Pits Nature Reserve

Ely

From Barton Square **A** go through the Porta archway, and take the second left before the park. Go behind the Cathedral and through the Sacrist Gate. Turn right into the High Street, and cross the Market Place. Go between Tesco and Archers Solicitors into Brays Lane. At the next road junction, turn right into Prickwillow Road and continue, crossing Lisle Lane, then coming to The Common.

Go through the kissing gate **B** onto The Common, and follow the path parallel to the B1382 road until you reach the sailing club. After passing the club, follow the track to the right. Cross the railway with caution **C** [556811] and head E. Cross the next railway line at a stile with extreme caution – fast trains and blind corner.

Queen Adelaide

Take the track on the left to the road **D**, turn right over the level crossing in Queen Adelaide village, and at the river bridge take the footpath on the W side of the river heading NE.

The path continues between the river and railway on an embankment; at the first stile by the railway **E** [568825] cross the railway and follow a track W over another rail crossing **F** [562823] which shortly joins the Bishops Way path.

Ely

Turn left and follow the waymarked track until you reach the
Prickwillow road **G**. Go along the road until you reach the
sailing club; retrace your steps across The Common, but at
Lisle Lane turn left and take the first footpath on the right
behind the bungalows and sheltered housing to Vineyards
Road. Continue along this until you reach the Market Place,
then return to Barton Square **A**.

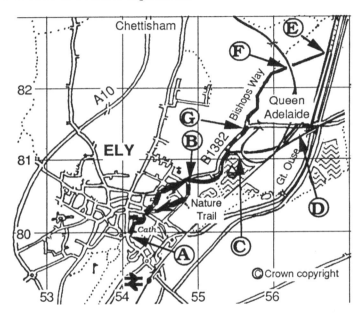

9 Ely – short walks

a Nature trail   2.5 miles / 4 kilometres
b River bank   3.5 miles / 5.5 kilometres
c Golf course   2 miles / 3 kilometres

Start: Ely, Barton Square **A** [540800]
Maps: Landranger 143; Pathfinder 941, 961

Ely

From Barton Square **A** cross the road towards the cathedral
and go through the monastic gateway called the Porta. Turn
second left before reaching the park and follow the path
around the E of the cathedral. Turn right through the Sacrist
Gate and right again into the High Street. You will soon come
to the market square on your left. Cross this diagonally and
leave via The Vineyards on your right, next to Archer & Archer
solicitors. The road name is not immediately apparent, but if
you pass the No Through Road sign you are on course.

At the bottom of The Vineyards turn right, then immediately
left, down a footpath which runs behind some bungalows.
Continue in the same direction across a road to another
footpath, marked Nature Trail. When you come to a wide road,
Lisle Lane, cross it and climb over the stile ahead. This gives
access to a permitted path which goes diagonally to your right
down the slope. This leads to another stile which is followed
by a path round the pits, now used for fishing and sailing.
Keep on this path until you reach a gate. Go through and turn
right onto a tarmac road. Just before the railway crossing **B**
there is a choice of route:

a Nature trail

Turn right through the kissing gate and follow the path back
to Lisle Lane, retracing your steps via the bungalows and The
Vineyards to the cathedral.

b River bank

Cross the railway with caution, and follow the road through
the Water Authority premises, keeping the buildings on your
right. Pass through a kissing gate ahead and follow a Public
Footpath sign over a footbridge. After a further 300 yards the
path leads to an iron bridge over the river which you should

cross. Now turn right along the road. Just after a bend to the right you can join the top of the flood bank and follow it for just over a mile to a T-junction **C**. Turn right again and cross back over the river by the Ely High Bridge. Turn right onto the towpath and follow it to the Cutter Inn. Just before you reach the pub take a footpath on your left to Broad Street. Turn right and after just 50 yards, cross the road and go through iron gates into the park. Follow the path back up beside the cathedral meadows to the Porta and Barton Square.

c Golf course

From Barton Square **A**, take the footpath signposted on the S of the square, by the Kings School/Barton Farm sign. Take the track alongside the playing field (on your left). When you reach a junction of paths by some allotments turn left. Follow this permitted path around the allotments. At the next corner turn right and then soon left, over a plank bridge. Now take the right hand fork towards some warehouse buildings. Just before the buildings turn right onto a footpath. This first runs alongside a playing field, then alongside crops. Just before the Ely bypass road ahead follow signs for a permitted path on your right. This path takes you onto the golf course. Please make sure that you keep to the signposted paths – and do look out for poor shots! The path initially skirts the golf course, then takes a route between fairways. Eventually you will come to a wooden gate **D**. Go through it and take the right hand path back past the allotments to Barton Square.

Cambridgeshire County Council 'Cawdle Fen' leaflet extends walk 'c' south to Little Thetford.

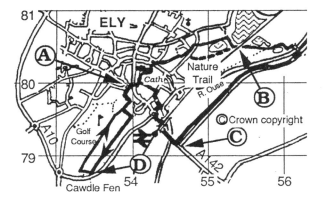

10 Haddenham circular

a skirting Haddenham 11 miles / 18 km
b through Haddenham 13 miles / 21 km

Start: Wilburton, Carpond Lane **A** [483749]
Maps: Landranger 143, (154); Pathfinder 961
Transport: Bus – from Cambridge to Wilburton and Haddenham
Refreshments: Wilburton – Kings Head PH
Haddenham – Three Kings and Cherry Tree PH
Aldreth – **no PH**

Points of interest:
Causeway and High bridge – old route onto the Isle of Ely
A booklet on the wildlife of the area is on sale in Haddenham

Wilburton

From Carpond Lane **A**, walk E along the main road towards Stretham for about 350 yards. Turn left into Station Road, passing the imposing Manor House on your left and the Recreation Ground on your right. After a quarter of a mile turn left into Broadway. As this road veers to the left after a further 300 yards, turn right into Hinton Way. At first stony, the track soon becomes grassy as it passes between hedges laden with blackberries in the autumn. Keep on the track as it swings right, ignoring a Public Footpath sign on a stile to your left.

The track meets up with Station Road again at the site of the former station. Go straight ahead on the road for a good half mile. At the junction with the Wentworth/Haddenham road turn left and continue along the road, keeping to the Haddenham signs and ignoring a right turn to Wentworth.

About 250 yards past a house on your left the road turns sharp left **B**; take a byway, Pingle Lane, straight ahead. This grassy track soon passes through high hedges and then trees. After 1000 yards the lane meets a farm track and then the A1421 main road. Turn right and cross the road, taking a metalled roadway to the left after 100 yards. There are often caravans parked here.

After 100 yards turn left onto a track which then crosses the 'New Cut Drain' – your companion from now on for much of the walk. There is a good grassy track on the right bank. Follow this. On your right you can see Sutton across the fields, with its marvellous church tower raised like a second Ship of the Fens, almost rivalling Ely Cathedral for bravura.

Keeping the New Cut Drain on your left you now have a pleasant grassy track as your path for the next 2 miles. You pass a number of barns noted on the map as individual farms, but none now inhabited. At the last, Galls Farm, the track swings left and becomes stony as it approaches the main A1123 Earith road **C**.

At the road you have now walked 5 miles. Cross it and turn left, then immediately right, keeping to a track on the right of the New Cut Drain. After 1000 yards you meet a surfaced track. Cross this and go up onto the bank ahead, still keeping the Drain on your left. Your route swings right, Fen Side on the Pathfinder map, which you follow S to Aldreth. After 400 yards the track swings left, then sharp right after a further 200 yards. If you want a look at Aldreth village, take Tinker's Lane to the left when you come to a junction 450 yards further on. Otherwise, keep to the right of the Drain.

The track swings to the left 500 yards past the Tinker's Lane junction, possibly becoming more overgrown, soon passing an agricultural machinery depot on the left bank of the Drain. When you come to a gravelled track join it – but keeping the same line, past the entrance to the depot. Abandoned machinery is littered along the route until you join the public highway – with 30 mph signs to your left near the entrance to the village. After a further 200 yards, where the metalled road turns sharp right, go left, onto another track, still alongside the Drain!

Haddenham

After a mile you have the option of going into Haddenham village, adding an extra 2 miles onto the distance. If you want to pass Haddenham by then skip both this and the next paragraph – just keep on the track until you meet a metalled road coming down from Haddenham village. But if you want refreshments, shops – and in the autumn excellent cheap apples from the many orchards in the area – then follow the Public Footpath sign by a footbridge on your left **D** – 9 miles so far. Keep along a field boundary (hedge on your right) until you meet a cross track. On the other side your route continues through an orchard until you pass through a kissing gate and garden and follow the track to the road. Turn right and walk up the hill (yes!) into Haddenham. At the junction by the Three Kings Pub you can turn left. After 100 yards there is a very pleasant public garden on your left, complete with seat, which gives excellent views over the fens to the S – a good place for a stop.

Retrace your steps to the pub and cross straight over (back on the A 1123). After 150 yards turn right into the recreation ground and follow the right hand boundary into a metalled path. Cross the road ahead into a street called Cherry Orchard, and take a pedestrian path to the right just before the road itself swings to the left. Follow this path round until it comes onto a road. Turn left and walk downhill out of Haddenham. After about 750 yards you meet up again with the track by New Cut Drain.

If coming from the track by the Drain turn right onto the metalled road – and if coming down from Haddenham swing left with the road after it crosses the Drain. 50 yards further on turn left away from the road, which turns sharp right. This track is called Fen Side. Soon after the unmistakeable poultry houses on your right you come to the B1049 Cottenham-Wilburton Road **E**. Cross this – first right then immediately left – picking up a stony track called Cut Bank on the Pathfinder map. But you're still alongside the Drain!

In under half a mile you are nearing what looks like a former Nissen hut on your right. Just before you reach it, take a track which turns off to your left, Mill Field Lane. Follow this N past Mitchell's Farm to the Wilburton/Stretham road. Turn left. There is a pavement on the right-hand side. This soon brings you back into Wilburton village.

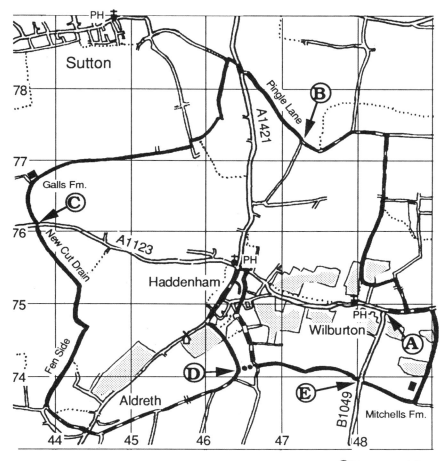

© Crown copyright

11 Stretham circular – shorter

5 miles / 8 kilometres

Start: Stretham church **A** [511746]
Maps: Landranger 143, 154; Pathfinder 961
Transport: Bus – from Cambridge or Ely
Refreshments: Stretham – fish and chip shop, PH
Points of interest:
> Stretham – restored perpendicular church, windmill,
> cross AD 1400
> Stretham Old Engine – 1831 fen pumping station,
> entrance fee

Stretham

Take the footpath just beyond the house on the N side of the church (on your left) **A**. The Public Footpath sign is set back from the road; at the time of writing the way leads through an open-sided shed! Follow the waymarks as the path continues W to cross the A10 Cambridge/Ely road. Now follow the field edge path past two fields. After the second plank bridge and stile, turn half right and cross this grassy field diagonally to the opposite corner. In the next field continue due N along a field edge until you come to a T-junction with a broad earthen track. Turn left. 300 yards further on you will come to a second T-junction. Turn left again to walk due S until you come to a road. Here you turn right – there is a pavement.

Now look for a track leading left, just before a line of cypress trees **B**. Cross the road and take the track – Red Hill Drove on maps. The path now leads S to Red Drove Farm. The route through the farmyard is not immediately obvious, but make for the silos; follow waymarks to pass them so they remain on your left, and then turn immediately right, W, into a broad green lane. This track – still Red Hill Drove – soon swings left and continues SE until it meets the A10 again.

When you reach the layby off the A10 turn left. Keep to the grass verge on this very busy road and cross the road opposite a garage on the other side. Now take the track to the right just before the garage forecourt **C**. After 600 yards, you will reach a wooden bridge on your left and here you have a choice of routes.

a

Follow the path over the bridge back to the village. If you choose this option continue until you meet a T-junction of paths near some houses. Turn right until you come to a lane. Now turn left and you will soon come into the village proper. At the next road junction turn right and almost immediately left, into Chapel Street. This will bring you back to the High Street by the church.

b

Continue along the track to a road **D**. Turn right and continue down Green End Road, a quiet lane, towards the Great Ouse river and the Stretham Pumping Station of 1831 **E**. This is clearly visible on your left and is reached by turning left once you have crossed the river bridge. The station contains some huge boilers and engines and is open all day from dawn to dusk for a modest fee. You can then retrace your steps and keep on back down the lane, Green End Road, into the village.

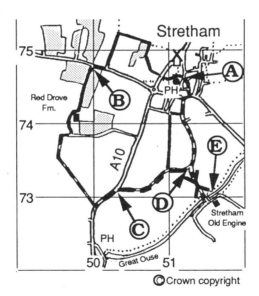

©Crown copyright

12 Stretham circular – longer

9 miles / 14.5 kilometres

Start: Stretham church **A** [511746]
Maps: Landranger 143, 154; Pathfinder 961
Transport: Bus – from Cambridge or Ely
Refreshments: Stretham – fish and chip shop, PH
                    Halfway round route – Lazy Otter PH

Points of interest:
    Stretham – restored perpendicular church, windmill,
        cross AD 1400
    Stretham Old Engine – 1831 fen pumping station,
        entrance fee
    Little Thetford – thatched round house
    Riverside stretches – river craft, birds
    Fen crops

Stretham

From the bus shelter **A** outside the church, turn left in front of
the church, noting the old Market Cross and the Red Lion inn
on the right. Turn right up Top Street. At the T-junction turn
left up Wood Lane and bear right at school. Beyond the end of
the houses, turn left on a signposted path along a
gravel/earth farm track **B** [516748].

At the pumping station, follow the track round to the right –
this is an agreed permissive route, instead of a right of way
over several fields. At the end of the large field on the left,
follow the track round to the left towards and beyond a
solitary tree – the Burying Way, originally used to carry coffins
from Little Thetford to the nearest church at Stretham. Later,
note the young trees planted on the adjacent bank of the
dyke.

Little Thetford

Continue, entering the outskirts of Little Thetford up a
hedged, hard-surfaced track. Before reaching the village, take
the first track on the left for 30 yards, then turn right on a
wide grassy track. On reaching Little Thetford Main Street,
turn right. Note St. George's church on the right, and the
thatched round-house on the left.

Ignore the signed footpath on the left **C**, but continue past the stables, to turn right in front of a black corrugated iron construction, on a mud track – Holt Fen Drove. Where a bridge spans the dyke on the right, do not cross it, but turn left up a broad grassy track with young trees on its left-hand side. Walk towards the railway line seen in the distance. One field before the line, follow the track round to the right, and then eventually to the left towards the railway.

Just in front of the railway **D**, take a U-turn sharp right along the bank of the river Great Ouse, with the river on the left. Cross a waymarked stile, and continue along the flood-bank. At the road, cross a stile and turn left. Cross the river on the road bridge – Military Bridge – taking care with traffic on the narrow carriageway.

Description continued overleaf

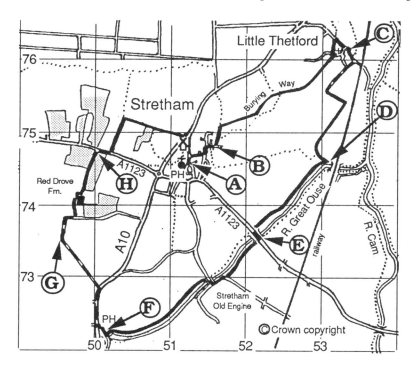

Over the bridge **E** [521737] turn right over the stile and onto the river bank; follow this towards Stretham Old Engine, crossing three more stiles, to meet the road. After visiting the Old Engine if you wish, walk up the lane and cross the river on the road bridge – Wooden Bridge. Turn immediately left over a stile, into a field on a signposted path, labelled 'Warning: Bull in Field'. Walk along the flood bank, crossing five stiles, to reach The Lazy Otter PH **F**.

Lazy Otter

Refreshed, leave The Lazy Otter and turn right along the road verge of the A10, passing Elford Farm. Cross the road to the layby, and take the signposted footpath over a stile. Follow the grass track – Red Hill Drove – which bends half-right at **G** [496735], and approach the farm, turning right with the track.

Just before farm buildings, turn left (waymarked) through the hedge, passing to the left of a railway-sleeper silage clamp. After 100 yards, turn right by the byre, and shortly left to follow the waymarked track by the hedge. (The right of way here is actually under the tall silos!) Continue along the track, with poplar trees on the left, following it round bends and past an orchard on the left, to a signpost at the Stretham – Wilburton road **H**

Cross the A1123 onto the footway and turn right. After 200 yards turn left by a Public Byway sign, onto Parson's Drove. At the top of the hill (height 15 metres!), turn right along another drove – Mill Way. At its end, cross the A10 with great care by the windmill. Turn right into Ely Road, Stretham, and walk back to the church and bus stop.

The droves hereabout may not be public; some have only been recently registered as rights of way, and may not be shown as such on some Ordnance Survey maps.

*Cambridgeshire County Council 'Cawdle Fen' leaflet extends this walk from **C** to Ely.*

13 Isleham – Worlington circular

10.5 miles / 17 kilometres

Start: Isleham priory **A** [643744]
Maps: Landranger 143, 154; Pathfinder 962
Refreshments: Isleham – PH, shops, fish & chips
                    Judes Ferry Bridge, Worlington,
                    Freckenham – PH

Points of interest:

Isleham Priory – well-preserved 11th century Romanesque church (English Heritage)

Isleham

Go E past the Priory **A** and church. Immediately beyond the church take the first left, Church Lane. Just before a T-junction there is a Public Footpath and Byway sign; turn right along an asphalt path running beside the byway. At the next junction with a minor road, turn left. After half a mile, where the road forks, go right, following another Public Footpath sign into Isleham Marina. Take the bridge over the river and turn left, keeping close to the river bank. Now keep the river on your left as you follow the path, crossing two wooden bridges, skirting around the marina. You will soon come to the junction with the River Lark at Isleham Lock **B**. Cross the metal bridge over the river and turn right. You will now follow the bank of the River Lark as far as Worlington – about 3.5 miles.

Keep to the path along the river bank when side tracks divert to the left **C**; if the path is overgrown, see the alternative route described later. However, where the official Right of Way has been diverted you will have to walk around one riverside property, Gravel Gardens – just follow the Footpath signs. About 2.5 miles along the bank the path skirts a smallholding and then enters the car park of Judes Ferry pub. You come onto the West Row/Freckenham Road at this point **D**.

Turn right, cross the road and then pick the riverbank path up again on your left, just before the road bridge. Around one mile further on you come to a large house – Kings Staunch Cottage on the map. At this point our route leaves the Lark. Follow the waymarks through a gate into a garden, then cross the footbridge – right – into a field **E**.

Worlington

The cross-field path now runs diagonally to your left. It goes through the hedge onto a track, where you should turn left. The track soon swings right, towards the church and village of Worlington. When you reach the church turn left into the churchyard through a kissing gate. Follow the path, first past the church then swinging right next to a cottage. As the path emerges into a lane look out for a cemetery on your left. Your route now goes through a gate to follow a path through the cemetery. This soon leads through to the Freckenham / Mildenhall Road. When you reach the road turn left.

Continue on the pavement though the village until you come to The Walnut Tree pub. Now cross the road and turn right. After 200 yards, just beyond the village speed limit signs, turn right down a sandy track. This passes through typical heathland for about a mile and a half until it meets Elms Road **F**. At this junction turn right and walk a further mile along the road into Freckenham. Turn right at the T-junction near the church and at the junction with the Mildenhall road keep straight on. Just past the next junction, with the Chippenham Road, turn right into Mortimer Lane **G**. Keep straight ahead after 500 yards when the main track turns left into a field. At the next field boundary the path swings first right, then left, leading up to Beck Bridge on the Isleham / Worlington road.

When you get to the new road turn left. There is generally little traffic on this road, but take care as you will have to follow it for much of the rest of the walk back into Isleham. After three-quarters of a mile you can take a right fork – Sheldrick's Road – to give you an opportunity to look round this fen edge village. Otherwise continue as far as the junction with The Causeway, where you should turn left, back past the church.

Summer alternative

Nettles can be a real problem between Gravel Gardens and Kings Staunch Cottage – luckily there is a good alternative route, shown as a broken line on the map.

Where the Gravel Drove diverts left from the river bank **C**, follow it, passing Gravel Gardens and continuing as a metalled track into the village of West Row. By the church, turn right, S, on a signposted footpath beside a bungalow. This continues as a grassy track across fields to the road just N of Judes Ferry bridge and PH – 100 yards on your right.

Retrace your steps from the pub, walking first N, then E as the road swings to the right. At a crossroads, continue ahead along Bargate Road. Where this turns sharp left into Pott Hill Road, turn right along a signposted bridleway. After 100 yards this turns left, SE, along a grassy bank, not far from the river. After 900 yards or so turn right at the signpost by Kings Staunch Cottage, rejoining the main route to cross the river **E**.

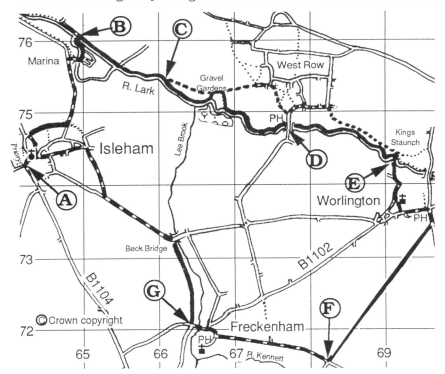

14 Soham circular

8 miles / 13 kilometres

Start:	Soham, St. Andrew's church **A** [593731]
Maps:	Landranger 143,156; Pathfinder 961, 962
Transport:	Bus – from Ely/Newmarket/Cambridge
Refreshments:	Shade windmill – teas on Sunday
	Fountain, Angel, Cherry Tree PH, cafe

Points of interest:
> St. Andrew's church
> Downfields windmill, working, open every Sunday
> Commons – Soham has a greater area of these than any
> other English or Welsh town

Start at the entrance **A** to the churchyard (public convenience nearby) opposite the Fountain PH, and go left down Fountain Lane. When you get to Station Road, go to the right of the Angel PH through cycle barriers down a tarmac footpath. When you reach Berrycroft, a metalled road, turn right. Take another tarmac path on the left, and turn left again along a track beside the allotments, going down the hill and out on Mereside. Turn left, and immediately right, across the railway to the river **B**.

Turn right along the river bank, straight across the first road – Middle Mere Farm – and turn right onto the second road – Pantile Farm. Recross the railway line and come out on The Cotes. Turn left and immediately right up Blackberry Lane, one of several in Soham! Carry on between the hedges until you come to what was Shade Common **C**, ploughed up during the Second World War and never returned to common use.

Turn right and follow the field boundary past the cottages up to the main road; the old Shade windmill is visible on your left, and you can make a detour for refreshments. Cross the main road out of Soham, logically called Townsend, and take the path alongside the hedge, Sayers Lake Drove. Turn right onto the next metalled road, Northfield Road; after 100 yards turn left on a track alongside another hedge, the continuation of Sayers Lake Drove. Follow it until the hedge ends **D**; if you reach Soham by-pass, you have gone 75 yards too far!

Turn right and proceed up the side of the field to reach a metalled road, Bancroft Lane. Turn right onto this until you see in front of you the wide open grassed area of Qua Fen Common, one of Soham's several commons. Cross the road and stand near the pond.

Follow the track winding along the boundary of the common, and take the path between houses, coming out on Bushel Lane. Turn left, then right at the pumping station, past the houses.

Head straight across the common to a derelict five-bar gate, go over the stile beside it, and straight across the next field, following the line of the telegraph poles. At the far end of this field a bridge over a ditch **E** leads to another common, East Fen Common.

Keep in a straight line parallel with the bypass across the common, past the single pole with a light on it, straight on down a track to come out at a new cattle grid across a metalled road. Cross the road and follow the track around the edge of the common, past a house on your left, and out onto the back of East Fen Common, climbing over the fence if the gate is locked in the summer.

Description continued overleaf

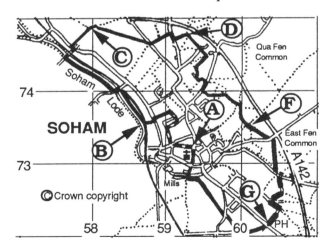

Cross the common diagonally to Loftus Bridge, in spring walking through a mass of buttercups and daisies. Cross the bridge and head down the drove in front of you. Where the housing starts, the track, called Greenhills, is metalled; carry on and take the first road left, bringing you out at the end of Brook Street. Turn left and follow the road round to the right past all the factories down Regal Lane to its end on the main Fordham Road **F**, with the Cherry Tree PH in front of you.

On a windy Sunday Downfields Windmill on your left may be working – well worth the small entrance charge.

Take the track beside the Cherry Tree PH, Cherry Tree Lane. Continue to a track on your right; turn there, passing the allotments on your right, straight across the first metalled road – the Butts – past the college playing fields and St. Andrew's School. Go straight across a new car park and down a concrete road past the Sports Hall to the river.

Turn left through the car park, then right over the river. Continue up College Road to a T-junction with Clay Street; on the far side of the road, slightly to your left, go through cycle barriers to a path between brick walls, which leads you back to the church **A**.

---

15 Wicken – Upware circular

2.5 miles / 4 kilometres

Start: Wicken, National Trust Car Park **A**
                [564705]
Maps: Landranger 156; Pathfinder 961, (982)
Transport: Bus – very infrequent, summer from
                    Cambridge and Ely
                Car – National Trust Car Park (payment)
Refreshments: Wicken – PH, few shops
                Upware – Five Miles from Anywhere PH
Points of interest:
        Remnants of original fen
        Nature Reserve

From the car park entrance **A** follow the road towards Wicken Fen; in a very few yards turn right and follow a broad grassy drove around the outer edge of Wicken Fen.

Where the drove turns right, go over the stile on the left. Follow another grassy drove along the edge of a dyke on the left. Over the dyke you will see examples of the original fen in the area, much higher than the ground on the right. Upon reaching the road **B** cross over to a well-defined field footpath; when you reach a hedge turn right and very soon left. At the drove turn left, passing Commissioners pit on the right, a nature reserve used by local schools. At the end of the line of trees turn right and then left around the edge of a field. When you reach a Marina cross a stile on your left into a field and continue until you reach a bridge and stile onto a road.

Turn right along the road which takes you past the Five miles from Anywhere PH. Keeping the river on the right, follow the footpath away from the pub along the bank of the river until Upware Lock is reached. Do not cross the river here, but turn left and follow the towpath along the edge past moorings and over a footbridge **C**. Turn left and follow Wicken Lode, keeping the water to your left. When you reach a planked bridge, cross it and turn left, the path then bears right and goes past the entrance of Wicken Fen, and the car park **A** is a few yards on your right.

The walk can be extended to Wicken village.

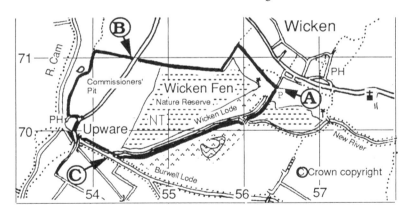

16 Fordham circular

3 miles / 5 km

Start: Fordham church **A** [633708]
Maps: Landranger 154; Pathfinder 962
Transport: Bus – Newmarket – Ely service
Refreshments: Fordham – The Crown, The Chequers PH
Points of interest:
  Fordham – church of St. Peter & St. Mary Magdalen,
    interesting double nave with belfry to one side.
  Open fen-edge landscape merging into Breckland, and
    crossed by the attractive, clear stream of the River
    Snail.

*Light sandy soil and tarmac inner-village paths provide an easy
surface in almost all weathers (though one narrow section by
the river could be slippery if wet). Section E – G shared with the
County Council's leaflet walk 'The Fordham – Isleham Railway
Line'.*

From the churchyard entrance **A** go S through the
churchyard, passing the church on your left. Follow the
tarmac path past a sunken graveyard, ignoring a side-turning
on the right, and continue between garden fences to emerge
on a residential road. Turn right (W) for about 50 yards, and
look for another tarmac path on the corner, continuing ahead
between houses nos. 20 and 21. Drop downhill, cross a road,
and continue on Ironbridge Path, beside a massive old clunch
wall, to cross the River Snail by a decorated iron bridge under
overhanging trees **B**.

Continue along the tarmac path, crossing an old mill-leat by a
second, more utilitarian bridge, to pass between hedged fields.
At the end of the first field take a right turn, also on a tarmac
path between hedges, and leading towards the car park of a
small industrial development. After passing a derelict
Primitive Methodist chapel and a street-sign 'New Path', the
path meets a road. Turn right here, and follow the road round
a left-hand bend, passing between industrial units, to reach
the main street by the village pump and seat, close to The
Chequers PH.

Turn left along the main street, crossing the road and bearing right after 100 yards along Carter Street. Opposite house number 121, look for a Public Footpath sign on your right, pointing down a hedged path **C**.

Follow this path for 100 yards, turning half-left (N) at the end of the hedge, where a white sign indicates 'Footpath'. The right of way should be reinstated across the arable land, but if the line is not clear head just left of an isolated power-pole in the middle of the field. An old gate indicates the crossing point into the next field, where you continue in a direction slightly W of N, towards a finger-post which can be seen on the road ahead **D** [627714]. At the road turn right, and walk for about 150 yards, round a corner and towards an isolated bungalow **E**.

To visit the nature reserve and the County Council walk along the track of the former Isleham railway, continue N for a further 500 yards; otherwise turn sharp right by another footpath sign just before the bungalow, to follow a narrow path between the garden hedge on your left, and the River Snail. Continue beyond the garden, still following the river which runs clear on its gravelly bed between steep banks.

Description continued overleaf

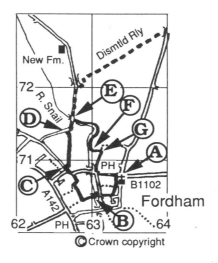

The path becomes a headland, somewhat overgrown by weeds, but easy to follow. After about 200 yards the river turns sharp right (S): the right of way here may still be shown on maps leaving the bank here to run slightly E of S across the arable field, but has been diverted to follow the good headland path beside a tall hedge which now lines the river bank, for a further 200 yards to meet a paddock fence **F** [629712].

Here turn left beside the fence, following it for 100 yards to a corner, then leaving it to continue ahead along a weedy strip between two arable fields. After a further 100 yards you will reach the corner of a tall hedge bounding the recreation ground **G** [631712] with a public convenience.

Look for a gap in the hedge a few yards to the right, and pass through into the playing field. Turn right and follow the edge of the field S, with trees and hedge on your right, eventually making for a gate to the left of the sports pavilions. Cross the gravelled car park, with a bowling green on the left and toilets to the right, and turn left along Church Street, passing the War Memorial and The Crown public house, to return to the church.

17 Snailwell – Fordham – Landwade circular

8 miles / 13 kilometres

Start: Snailwell village green **A** [645675]
Maps: Landranger 154; Pathfinder 962, 983
Transport: Bus – Newmarket – Fordham – Ely service
Refreshments: Snailwell – George & Dragon PH
                   Fordham – The Crown, The Greyhound PH

Points of interest:
Snailwell village sign
Chippenham Fen nature reserve
Landwade Hall and church

Snailwell

If parking by the village green first walk about 200 yards along the road leading to Exning. Opposite Snailwell Stud take the broad track on your right **A**, marked with a Public Footpath sign. You should have an open field on your left and a historic brick wall on your right. At the end of the wall, there is a field with paddock fencing. Pass this by and you will soon pass alongside a second paddock field. At its end, turn right into the field, crossing over a stile. You will see Snailwell Church about 150 yards ahead of you. At the other side of the field you will need to cross a second stile.

Continue down the gravel track past the very attractive Church with its round flint tower. Some fine period houses in the vicinity are well worth a look. At the road ahead turn left, going past the George & Dragon pub. After about 300 yards take a track with Public Footpath sign to your right, and proceed for about 150 yards between high hedgerows. As you come into a large field beyond, make a slight turn towards the left.

Take the vehicle track running on to a tall hedgerow some 500 yards ahead. Passing through the hedge and tree belt you will continue in a field with a slight embankment immediately on your right. Follow this track for a further 500 yards and you will come to a crossing of several routes at the corner of woodland **B**. Turn left at right angles and walk along a track with the wood on your right and a white gate straight ahead. On reaching the gate you are now entering . . .

Chippenham Fen

Chippenham Fen is a National Nature Reserve and a display board by the gate provides some information on the area. Our route goes straight ahead – walking is very pleasant through Jerusalem Wood and the Fen. After about 500 yards you will see a dark wooden gate ahead – but there is a stile on the right which you should step over. Continue in the same direction for about 200 yards across more open fen until you reach a belt of trees.

There is a clear footpath running across your route and you should turn left, keeping the trees and fence on your right. You now walk in woodland for about 350 yards until you come to a stile ahead. Cross over and turn right on a well defined path which soon becomes a proper track. You will now have a hedgerow on your left. Looking along the slightly rising track ahead you can see Fordham Church, with its square tower. Just before a large barn, by a grassy field, the track swings to the right for about 100 yards, to a T-junction with a track known as the King's Path. Turn left and walk through Trinity Hall Farm to the road beyond **C**.

Fordham

Here you have a choice. You can either go straight ahead at the road for about 500 yards, then right for about 60 yards to turn left down Station Road by the Greyhound pub, shown as a broken line on the map. Alternatively, you can spend a little while looking at some of Fordham village, including the Church. If you take this course, turn right out of the farmyard. Walk along the pavement until you pass the church on your left. Turn left at the crossroads (with the B1102) – you will see the primary school opposite. You are now in Church Street. Pass the Crown pub on your right. After about 300 yards turn left down Mill Lane – opposite a recreation ground with public conveniences. [4 miles]

After a further 300 yards you will see a tarmac path to your right, called Ironbridge Path. About 30 yards on you will indeed cross a very ornate iron bridge – and see a number of other bridges leading from nearby back gardens. Follow along this path, first between trees, then hedges and open fields and then houses. At the road junction by a telephone box, turn left and then immediately right – by the Greyhound pub. You are now in Station Road.

Walk along the footpath on the road side for about 400 yards. You will soon see a Public Footpath sign on your left. Follow the track, at first between high hedges. Soon the landscape opens out on your right to a series of fields – with a hedge and ditch on your immediate left.

About 15 yards away from the apparent dead end in the fourth such field you should look to your left. There is a bridge over the ditch made out of two old railway sleepers. On the other bank of the ditch should be a low post complete with yellow waymarks. Cross the bridge and turn right. Now continue along the field headland with the hedge on your right. About 150 yards ahead is the Ely/Newmarket railway – and you must cross it, using the gates provided to gain access to the track.

Description continued overleaf

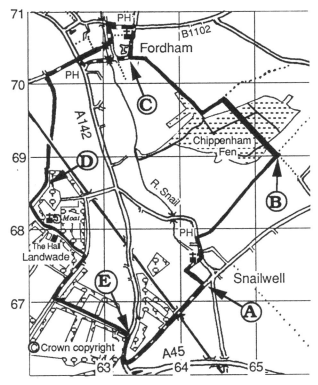

Once across the line your route continues in a similar direction to that taken so far from Fordham. You need to take a half turn from the railway – so you move gradually away from the line itself. The reinstated track leads over to the tree belt ahead, where you must search out a path just inside the wood, newly created by the landowner. This runs first to the right, W, then at the corner of the woodland it turns left, S, again following the edge but just inside the trees. After 200 yards or so you will need to climb over a wooden fence into a drive way.

Landwade

You are now in the vicinity of Landwade Hall and estate. Walk over the track which crosses your path and go through a silver-coloured metal gate ahead **D**. You are now on a tarmac driveway. After a few yards you will see a small lake on your left, complete with geese and ducks if you are lucky. Follow the drive as it turns quite sharply to the left. At a junction, do not turn right past a large barn, but instead follow the track to the left. You will see an old church to your left in a grassy field. Enter the field and keep straight on, with a fence and hedge on your right. Ahead is an attractive cast-iron park fence with kissing gate. Go through the gate. Immediately ahead you can now see Landwade Hall.

Your destination is behind the Hall. After coming through the gate in the park fence turn left along a mown grass path. Then, when you have passed the church once more (on your left), you should turn right along a further mown grass track, coming into the gravelled drive/car park behind the Hall. Make sure that you keep the Hall buildings on your right at all times. When you come into the drive area, turn slightly left and you will see a long tarmac roadway ahead. Take this and walk down to the Landwade Road, where there should be a Public Footpath sign. [6 miles]

Turn right and for the next 550 yards you will be walking along a road. However, the grass verge is broad and a path is clearly marked out, off the roadway itself. About 300 yards after passing a minor road on your right take a broad vehicular track on your left, which is a Public Footpath. Next to a metal gate there is a separate kissing gate for pedestrians. There is a small yellow waymark arrow on a telephone pole just inside the gate.

Walk along the track to its end – about 700 yards. Where it fades out, turn left and after about 30 yards right. You are now in a large field. Follow the field edge, with a hedge on your right, down to the road below. This will probably be all too obvious because it is often very busy! At the corner of the field there is the choice of a metal gate or stile **E**. Turn right along the road. For most of the way you can keep off the carriageway itself – but this is easily the worst 300 yards of the excursion!

You now want to take the (quiet) Snailwell road, signposted to the left, just after the Exning turn. The noise of the nearby A45 is rather unpleasant at first – but you soon turn further to the left and, with close mown grass verges, this road is generally very pleasant to walk along. You pass Plantation Stud first, then cross a road bridge over the railway line. A further 500 yards brings you back into Snailwell village again.

18 Exning circular

7 miles / 11 km

Start: Exning, White Horse PH **A** [622658]

Maps: Landranger 154; Pathfinder 983

Transport: Frequent bus & train services to Newmarket from Cambridge or Bury St. Edmunds; walk along the A142 footway for about 1 mile to join the walk at **F**

Refreshments: Exning – White Horse PH

Points of interest:

    Various racing studs

    Landwade church

    Landwade Hall grounds – snowdrops and aconites in early spring

    Newmarket – Clock Tower, National Horseracing Museum.

Exning

Start in Exning village, by the White Horse PH **A** just N of the church. Go down Swan Lane, past the inn. The lane bends to the right at the junction with Chapel Street. When the road bends sharply left, go straight on along North End Road. Leaving the last houses and the farm on the left, climb a slight rise with fields on both sides. Beyond North End House the lane trends downhill to a cross-roads **B** [609671].

Here turn right and walk along an earth track, with an open field on the right and a hedge on the left. Nearby are traces of a dismantled railway. The track narrows and becomes restricted by hedges. After a few hundred yards it turns right at **C** onto the metalled Landwade road, by some houses.

Take the first turning left along a tarmac track through the gate towards Landwade Farm. You have just passed from Suffolk into East Cambridgeshire! Go straight on, passing the farm house on your left, and beyond the outbuildings, continue on an earth farm track. Turn right in front of a tree-topped bank – Earthwork on the Pathfinder map – ignoring the track going off to the left. Follow the field boundary and up another track through the belt of trees.

Landwade Hall

Go through the metal gate into the pasture ahead, noting the isolated Landwade church to the left **D.** Continue forward E through the field, to leave it by a metal kissing gate. Just beyond this, note the ornamental stone seat on the edge of lawns to the rear of Landwade Hall. Turn left and walk across the grass (may be a mown strip), to meet a crossing track leading to the church. Turn right, going through a white wooden gate, and leave the grounds of the Hall by turning slightly left and down the drive, towards the ornamented bridge. Go on down the long entrance drive, and at the lodge **E** [628676] turn right to walk along the wide grass verge towards Exning.

Description continued overleaf

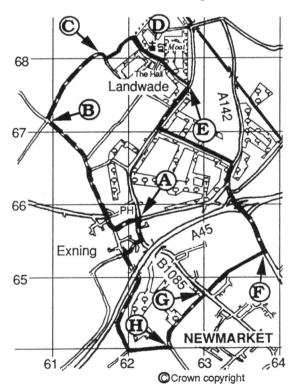

©Crown copyright

Pass a turning on the right leading back to Landwade, and continue forward on Cotton End Road for 250 yards. Turn right to go through a kissing gate beside a larger field gate, and along a track running along the right side of stud fields, with a belt of trees to your right. Carry on beyond the end of the track by dipping down into a shallow depression, partly filled with tree stumps, and go on along a rough grass strip on the right side of an arable field. Turn right on the A142 road to Newmarket by the former Isolation Hospital buildings.

Newmarket

Continue towards Newmarket, crossing a bridge over the bypass, and passing the residential Studlands Park Estate on the right. At 200 yards beyond Studland Park Avenue **F** turn right by a garage, and walk down the road through the works yard of the caravan manufacturers and caravan storage area. When the road stops, continue forwards along a narrow path which leads down over a small stream and gradually up a slope onto the B1045 Newmarket/Exning road **G** [630648].

Cross the road to Hamilton Road, almost directly opposite, running between horse pastures lined with scots pine trees. The road passes Hamilton Stud and further buildings, then swings right. At **H** [626640], turn right by a notice 'Private Road to Waterworks' (this is, in fact, a public byway). The track turns right by a pumping station and leads to the bypass, where turn right to follow a path screened by wicker fencing. Walk alongside the A45 to reach a tunnel under the road. On emerging, bear slightly right and walk along a gravel track, passing fields and allotments, to reach Chapel Street in Exning. Turn right immediately and walk along Ducks Lane. At the road junction, turn left and walk back to your starting point.

19 Burwell circular

8 miles / 13 km

Start: Burwell Recreation Ground **A** [583674]
Maps: Landranger 154; Pathfinder 982
Transport: Bus – from Cambridge and Newmarket
Refreshments: Burwell – several PH

Turn left out of the Recreation Ground car park **A**, and walk along the river until you reach the last barn. Turn left and walk along the left bank of Burwell Lode for about 2 miles, where you come to a bridge across the river **B**. Cross over it and walk along the right bank of the lode until you reach the bridge **C** under which is Wicken Lode. Here turn right along Wicken Lode.

This is a delightful part of the walk, and if you are interested in birds you should take binoculars. Where New River joins the Lode **D**, turn right but do not go over the bridge – stay on the S side for about another 2 miles. Go under the pylons **E** and you come to a farm drive, but keep by the river for about half a mile until you come to a fence, where you should turn right. Keep the fence on your left. The path here is narrow, and there is a dyke on your right. The path runs by a house and then parallel to the farm track: it soon meets a road.

Continue along the road until you get to a T-junction by a sewerage works. Turn right and continue into Burwell. At the Anchor pub, turn right into Anchor Lane and cross the lode, to rejoin the original track. Turn left, back to the Recreation Ground.

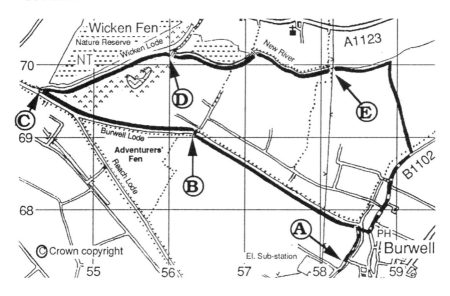

20 Reach – Burwell – Wicken circular

a 14 miles / 22 kilometres

b 11.5 miles / 18.5 kilometres

Start: Reach village green **A** [566662]

Maps: Landranger 154; Pathfinder 961, 982

Transport: Bus – occasional to Reach and Wicken, more regular to Burwell from Cambridge and Newmarket

Refreshments: Wicken – Maids Head PH
                   Burwell – several PH
                   Upware – Five Miles from Anywhere PH
                   Reach – The King's PH

Points of interest:

Devils Dyke
Reach conservation area, Reach Lode and port
Burwell Castle site – information board on site
Wicken Fen and Commissioners Pit nature reserves

Reach

From the village green **A** the first section of the walk is along the Devils Dyke. You join it at the S end of the green; it is well signed. A chalk path takes you right onto the Ditch between high hedges of hawthorn. After 1000 yards you come into a cleared section of path. You will see a wooden signpost pointing to the left down a flight of steps. Go down and follow the path between two fields. After the first field the path joins a broad grassy track which joins it from the left. Keep straight on until you come to the tarmac Reach Road.

Burwell

Cross the road and follow the footpath signpost arm marked Burwell. The well-used path crosses a field, following power lines. Across the field you cross a concrete bridge and then follow along a field edge with a ditch on your immediate left.

For a diversion you can turn right to explore the ancient site of Burwell Castle, but return to this point. You turn left **B** and cross a second ditch, veering immediately to the right so that you are walking along a field edge with a hedge on your right. When you come to the corner of the field you join a path running behind the back gardens of houses in Burwell.

Turn left; for the next 150 yards you are effectively skirting more back gardens. But the path doesn't run in a straight line and soon you have to turn left, then right and right again to regain your line. You should by now be by a barrier across the path – two metal poles which it is best to step through.

On the other side you find a grassed area in a small housing estate. Turn left, keeping a high hedge on your left. By the end house ahead you will see a tarmac path running straight on. Take it, past the edge of the housing estate. After about 200 yards you meet a ·gravelled path, soon running into Low Road, with a signpost pointing back to Reach and Swaffham Prior.

Continue along Low Road for about 550 yards, until you come to a T-junction. Turn left and go over the bridge after a further 200 yards. Turn right, keeping the stream on your right. Keep on, as the tarmac becomes a stony track past the recreation ground. Keep on through what appears to be a scrapyard, right up to the junction with Burwell Lode. Turn left – you can hardly go on unless you want a swim! – by a signpost pointing to Upware 3.5 miles. You have now walked almost 3 miles **C**.

Lodeside walking

The next 5 miles are along the sides of the ancient fen lodes. You begin with Burwell Lode. You can either walk on the lode dyke, with good views for miles, or keep to the track alongside. The dyke tops can be rather prone to stinging nettles and thistles, so shorts and short socks can lead to some discomfort in summer! After about 1.5 miles you will see a big footbridge over the lode **D**. Cross over.

Now you have a choice. A quick way into Wicken, shown as a broken line on the map, involves taking the track about 20 yards to the E of the footbridge. This passes Priory Farm and leads you in just over half a mile to Monk's Lode, just outside Wicken Village.

But if you want a good look at part of the Wicken Fen Nature Reserve, then turn left once over the bridge **D**. Keep along the lode, again either on the dyke top or along the nearby track. In summer the vegetation to your right is most interesting. This is Adventurers Fen, owned by the National Trust, and is looked after by them.

Description continued on next page

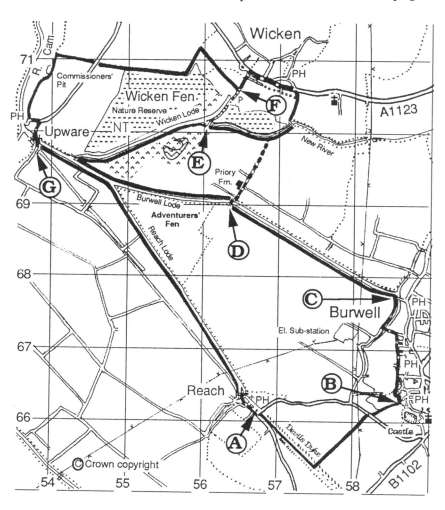

After a mile and a quarter you will see a steep footbridge ahead. Do not cross it, but turn right instead, along Wicken Lode. A National Trust sign tells you you are entering Wicken Fen. Cross the stile and keep along the well-mown lode edge. A mile further on you will come to another junction of waterways **E**. Again turn right. You are now walking along Monk's Lode. Cambridgeshire County Council have waymarked many of the routes round Wicken and their signs are displayed on stiles and signposts in the area.

Wicken

Do not cross the Monk's Lode, but keep it on your left. After half a mile your route drops off the lode dyke to meet a tarmac path coming in from the right – the shortcut from Priory Farm mentioned above. You soon cross the lode by a footbridge on the right, and keep on the path into Wicken village. You will see the Maids Head pub opposite, on the village green. If you don't want to walk along the village street – which is, after all, the A1123 – you can take a signposted footpath which runs behind the houses on the S side of the road for about 600 yards. You have now walked 8 miles, or 5.5 miles by the shorter route.

On reaching the main street, turn left and walk along it. Soon after the shop and post office you will see a brown National Trust signpost pointing left to Wicken Fen. Take this road. If you have extra time and energy you can now visit Wicken Fen (admission charge; car park; public conveniences).

Opposite the car park a broad track **F**, marked on the Pathfinder map as Breed Fen Drove, runs off to the right, just before a cottage; take it. You are now walking alongside part of the Trust's Nature Trail. After about 600 yards you meet another drove, Spinney Drove. The main drove swings right, but our route goes left. So cross the stile on your left and follow the drove round for almost 1 mile. There are often cattle grazing here. The new building you pass houses an engine which pumps water into the Fen when necessary.

When you come to a metal gate go through it onto the road. Take a signposted footpath on the other side of the road. The route then crosses an arable field due W. After one field you pick up a hedgerow on your left. You come into another broad drove, Fodderfen Drove, running across your route. Turn left and follow the drove to its end. You will pass by Commissioners Pit on your right, a nature reserve owned by Cambridgeshire County Council.

Where the drove ends, turn right and then left, so you keep to the track skirting the cropped field. There is a big lake to your right and the River Cam beyond it.

Upware

You are now walking into Upware village. Your path meets a track running across it near the marina. Turn left and then immediately right over a stile. You are now in a grassy field. Keep the hedge boundary to the marina on your right, and follow it across the field. There is a stile and footbridge on the other side, leading onto a road. The Five Miles From Anywhere PH is on your right.

Turn right and pass in front of the pub, picking up a path on the embankment ahead. This swings to the left, to the main village road. Turn right and walk down to the bridge over Burwell Lode **G**. Cross the road bridge and then turn left. You are now back on Burwell Lode, with the watercourse on your left. Again follow first Burwell and then Reach Lode back to your start. The path on the top of the dyke is generally clear for at least the first mile, but if the undergrowth defeats you, you can drop down to the track running alongside. It is now about 3 miles back to Reach.

After three-quarters of a mile the lodes divide and you have no choice but to keep right, following Reach Lode. A further 2 miles or so on, and the track turns sharp right away from the lode. Don't follow it, but regain the dyke top. After a few yards you will come into a field, frequently grazed by sheep. At the other side, again back on the dyke, you cross another stile and soon meet a track coming in from your right. You will see a footbridge on your left. Take it to cross the side-lode that you are on. You are now in Reach Port. A signboard explains the history.

Turn right and you are soon back in the village.

21 Swaffham Bulbeck walks

a Cow Bridge – Swaffham Bulbeck Green –
   Commercial End   1.5 miles / 2.5 km

b Cow Bridge – Docking & Cranney Droves –
   Longmeadow   3 miles / 5 km

c Cow Bridge – Lode 5 miles / 8 km

Start: Swaffham Bulbeck Cow Bridge **A** [553635]
Maps:
Transport: Bus – Cambridge – Burwell service
Refreshments: Swaffham Bulbeck – Black Horse PH, by
                        The Green
                        Lode – Three Horseshoes PH
                        Anglesey Abbey, 0.25 miles/0.5 km off the
                            route – National Trust restaurant/tea
                            room, normally open Easter – October
                            and Winter weekends

Points of interest:
   Village signs
   Windmills
   Swaffham Bulbeck, Commercial End – old buildings
   Anglesey Abbey and Lode Mill (National Trust)

a Cow Bridge – Swaffham Bulbeck – Commercial End

*Level with no stiles, suitable for the less able in dry
conditions*

At Cow Bridge **A** cross Swaffham Bulbeck lode and turn left
immediately on the signposted footpath (wide grass track) with
the stream on the left. After 200 yards turn right at the
signpost, following a narrow path with an arable field on the
left, and a ditch to the right. After a further 300 yards,
continue ahead on a narrow track between arable crops to the
signpost at Station Road **B**.

At the road, turn left along the verge towards the village green, and, beyond the 30 mph sign, turn half-left across the green, admiring the fine mature trees. By the road corner on the far side, beyond the childrens' swings, enter drive (a signposted public footpath), by a kissing-gate beside the entrance, which has distinctive white railings. Go along the drive, then continue forward on the grass between a grey corrugated-iron barn on the left, and a bungalow on the right, to exit at a second kissing gate **C**.

Turn left onto the minor road into Commercial End, passing a chapel on the right. Note the thatched and pantiled cottages (1730) and Victorian fire hydrant, and Old Malting House with shell doorway (1697). Avoid turnings down Mill Lane and Archers Close, but turn left down Fen Lane at the end of Commercial End. First pause, however, to look at the old house (North) in the field ahead: it contains the remains of an old Benedictine nunnery. Continue along Fen Lane, back to Cow Bridge **A**.

b Cow Bridge – Docking & Cranney Droves – Longmeadow

c Cow Bridge – Docking & Cranney Droves – Longmeadow – Lode

From Cow Bridge **A**, walk SW up the road for 250 yards to the first turning on the right, signed Red Tile Farm. Turn into this drove and, after only 50 yards, turn left by the green footpath signpost along a narrow gap between arable crops. Continue forward past the end of a ditch **D** and turn right at the next ditch to meet a second footpath sign at **E** [545633]. (The definitive right of way, which you may prefer to use, runs across the field directly between **D** and **E**). At **E**, turn left across a narrow grass baulk, then immediately right along an attractive wide green lane (Docking Droveway), running NW with bushes and trees on the left-hand side.

Continue past the farm entrance on the left, crossing the line of the former Cambridge/Mildenhall railway: only two stout gateposts and a length of old railway fencing remain here. Later, note new tree planting beside the path, at the end of which the drove terminates in a crossing dyke. Cross this dyke on an earth bridge **F** [538642].

The right of way (waymarked in yellow) continues ahead across the arable field to the corner, to another waymark post. Turn sharp left through the hedge, and turn back with hedge on left, and continue until you meet a crossing dyke, and another waymark. Here turn right. (You have just walked two sides of a narrow triangle, the base of the triangle is a 'permissive' short cut, waymarked in white on red, which you may use instead). For the permissive route, from **F** turn immediately left along the bank, with the dyke on the left. On meeting a tall crossing hedge, look for a narrow gap with a trodden track about 10 yards away from the dyke. The track crosses a shallow ditch **G** and rejoins the bank.

From **G** continue along the trodden field edge on a widening path, which becomes a 10 ft wide grassy track after about 500 yards. The track continues along the curving bank of the dyke to just short of the field corner. Here, turn left, crossing the dyke on an earth bridge, and join Cranney Drove, another broad grass lane, running SE between dykes. After 600 yards, pass the end of a line of poplars, and, shortly, follow the drove as it turns half-left recrossing the former railway track. Continue past a large Dutch barn and a cottage, both on the right. The track becomes a gravelled road, entering Longmeadow hamlet, with its single street.

Just before the first house on the left **H**, turn left along the stony road. After 250 yards, leave the road, where it turns left towards The Grange Farm, and continue forward on the grassy track to the signpost **E** encountered earlier. Retrace steps via **D** to Cow Bridge **A**.

Description continued overleaf

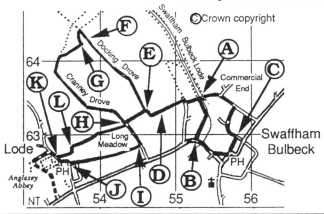

To extend the walk from Longmeadow to Lode, continue ahead from **H** along the street, then turn right (W) signposted between houses 35 and 37 **I** over a grassy area, to follow a tufty grass strip and later a low hedge between fields. After 400 yards the hedge ends, but keep the same direction across an arable field, aiming for a large gap in the line of houses visible ahead. At the end of the field there is once again a field boundary to follow, and shortly a grassy track which leads into Millards Lane, a residential cul-de-sac. Continue ahead to Lode Road **J**, then turn right to follow the road round left and right bends into Lode High Street.

If desired, a left turn into Chapel Lane leads into a network of waymarked footpaths by which the National Trust properties at Anglesey Abbey (admission charge) can be reached in about a quarter mile; but for the main walk continue along High Street to Lode Post Office **K** and turn right beside the churchyard, along Fassage Close. At the end of the close, pass to right of the houses on an asphalt path to the Recreation Ground (seats). Follow the path round to the right, passing the start of the 'National Playing Fields Association Family Fitness Circuit'. Turn left in front of a white pan-tiled cottage, and follow the narrow asphalt path round the perimeter of the Recreation Ground, and through a gap in the tall hedge **L**. The asphalt path continues E between open fields, to reach Longmeadow by an Anglian Water enclosure, whence turn left to reach **H** after a few yards, then right to return to Cow Bridge.

A Cambridgeshire County Council leaflet describes further walks to the W of Lode.

22 Stetchworth walks

a 2 miles / 3 km
b via Ditton Green – 3 miles / 5 km
c from Dullingham Station – 6 miles / 10 km

Start: a and b   **A** [641595] at crossing of minor road by Devils Dyke

      c   Dullingham station **G** [617585]

Maps: Landranger 154; Pathfinder 1005

Transport: **Rail** – infrequent train service to Dullingham Station

Refreshments: Stetchworth – The Marquis of Granby PH
      Ditton Green – The Three Blackbirds PH

Points of interest:
     Devils Dyke Ancient Monument (Earthwork from The Dark Ages with rich botanical interest)
     Extensive countryside views from the Dyke
     The route crosses Icknield Way Long Distance Path

Although the walk options are quite short, none is suitable for the less able, as the Dyke is often wet and slippery, and there are several places where it is necessary to climb over or around fallen trees.

From **A** take the path onto the Dyke signed 'Woodditton' and follow the narrow chalky track, taking care among overhanging trees and stumps. The Icknield Way Long Distance path crosses the route at a dip in the Dyke **B** [648589] halfway along the earthwork.

a
For the short walk, turn left NE across an arable field on a generally reinstated path to reach the track at Dane Bottom **E** and turn left to continue the walk description from there.

b

For the medium length walk, continue along the top of the Dyke, noting interesting chalkland flora, growing in the cleared area. The Dyke ends in an arable field **C**. Follow a grass track along the right-hand edge of an arable field, turning left along the backs of gardens, to emerge through a grassy passage between gardens, to emerge in Ditton Green **D**. (This recent diversion is not shown on older maps). (To visit the Three Blackbirds PH turn left along the road for 250 yards.)

Continue the walk by turning left along the road only 50 yards as far as the water tower. Then turn left again on a track in front of the water tower. Pass through two gates, towards stables. Just before reaching the stables, a mown grassy track veers half-right, then continues behind the stable yard, following wooden railings, to rejoin the hard track beyond the buildings. Pass through a white gate to leave the farm complex, and continue on the gravel track for about 300 yards to a junction of paths **E** [650591]. (Short route rejoins here). For both walks, continue NW along the gravel track to Court Barns **F**, where turn left along the quiet minor road to return to the start **A**.

c

From the station yard **G**, behind the signal box turn SE towards Dullingham village. At Eagle Lane **H** turn left up the lane to the B1061 **I**. A detour may be made from **H** to visit Dullingham village with attractive thatched cottages and PH.

Cross the B1061 to find a wooden signpost opposite, indicating a headland footpath with trees, and then hedges on the left, and arable crops to the right, for 2 fields. On reaching a paddock on the left, continue forward over a railing stile into the next pasture field, and out onto the road by a wooden signpost and turn left into Stetchworth village (Marquis of Granby PH is reached at T-junction).

Opposite the PH, take the signposted footpath running NE between garden fences. The path crosses a residential cul-de-sac, and continues between gardens in the same direction, emerging as a headland path with hedge on left and arable field on the right. Continue forward on the clear headland track aiming for the gap in the Dyke ahead **B**. Turn right at the dyke, and walk around the medium circuit described above – **C**, **D**, **E**, **F**, **A**.

From **A** continue SW along the road, to the cross-roads. Keep in the same direction along the quiet road, which passes through the centre of a small circular wood to return to Eagle Lane **I** (noting stone eagles on the gate posts of Dullingham House) and thence to Dullingham Station **G**.

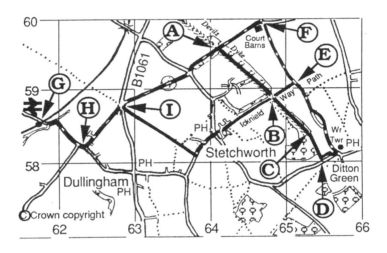

23 Ashley – Cheveley circular

6.5 miles / 10.5 kilometres

Start: Ashley village pond **A** [697616]
Maps: Landranger 154; Pathfinder 983
Transport: Bus – from Newmarket
Refreshments: Ashley & Cheveley – PH, shop and PO

From the village pond **A**, make your way to the High Street – the B1063 Clare Road – and walk S out of the village, past the Old Plough pub. At the brow of the hill take a cross-field path on your right which runs diagonally through crops to the edge of a wood. Continue on a field edge path to a minor road. There is a shallow ditch which requires some care in crossing.

Turn right (W) and continue along the lane past racing studs to housing by a village green. Go right diagonally across the green and follow a signposted path to the right. This grassy track goes between hedges and emerges at Brook Stud, Cheveley. Follow the road out of the stud and turn right by the green ahead **B**.

The route now follows the road through the attractive village of Cheveley for about a mile. For most of the way there is a pavement, but once over the cross-roads you will have to walk on the roadway itself. Go up the hill ahead. At Sandwich Stud turn left opposite a footpath sign and go through a small gate next to the main gate. First you pass a stable block and other buildings on your left. Continue along the road for about 300 yards until you come to a very distinctive stable block of red and white with a red tiled roof. At this point the road swings right – keep straight ahead, keeping two barns on your right. There is a path through the woodland strip, but it can be rather overgrown. After about 300 yards the path meets a broad grass track on the left. This now leads between the trees and paddock fencing. Turn left and then immediately right onto the track.

Just past a wooden barn on your left **C** turn right to a railed fence. You can slide the bottom bar along to gain access (please replace it). Go through the fence into an avenue of trees between paddock fencing. You will soon join a white gravel path. Keep the main stud buildings on your left. Carry on along the drive to the point where the road swings left. Turn right down a broad green track, keeping woodland on your left and paddock fences on your right.

Where the track turns right your route lies straight ahead, just inside a narrow belt of trees. There is a clear woodland track which you should follow until you reach a minor road. Cross straight over, picking up another track as far as a second road – the B1063 Ashley/Cheveley. Now turn left and follow the road back into Ashley.

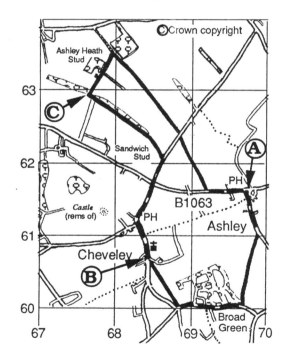

24 Ditton Green – Upend circular

9 miles / 14 kilometres

Start: Ditton Green **A** [660582]

Maps: Landranger 154; Pathfinder 983, 1005

Refreshments: Ditton Green – The Three Blackbirds PH
Cheveley – Red Lion PH
Kirtling, slightly off route – Red Lion PH

Ditton Green

From the main Stetchworth-Saxon Street road **A** walk NE in the Saxon Street direction. At the cross-roads turn right along the Kirtling Road for 350 yards. Turn left just before a belt of trees. Continue along a grassy track with first the trees, then a paddock fence, on your right. You soon join a hoggin track from your left. Keep straight on along the track until you pass through a wooden gate, just before a small wood on your left. This is a cross-roads of tracks. You turn right, keeping a hedge on your right and a paddock fence on your left. You keep on this track, which soon becomes a wide grassy lane, for around one mile.

When you come to Lucy Wood turn left onto a path which can be quite muddy. This passes just inside the wood for about 400 yards, first quite narrow and then broadening when it joins a track from the right. At the corner of the wood you can see a wooden bridge ahead on the right. Cross it, and pass through a kissing gate beyond. Now turn slightly left, following a path through the grass field to a gap in a hedge. Pass through and then turn slightly right. You are aiming for the flint cottage ahead, a former school. The path takes you to a stile at the road **B**.

Kirtling

Turn left, cross the road and then go right, opposite the Public Footpath signpost between the flint house and Kirtling Village Hall. About 20 yards down the lane you see a white cottage on your left. Pass it and take an old lane between high hedges (if overgrown follow the field edge on your right). After 120 yards, at the end, turn left and go through a gap in the hedge into the grassy field beyond. You can see the village sewage works ahead – and you head for them, keeping a hedge on your right. Pass to the right of the works onto the road. Turn right. You've walked about 2.5 miles so far.

After 200 yards on the road you can see a Public Footpath sign on your left, pointing along a grass track towards a small wood. Walk along this with a hedge on your left. Climb over the stile beside a gate into the wood and follow the narrow path cut through the trees. On the other side of the wood new tree planting has been recently carried out. Keep to the field edge with a hedge on your left as far as the copse ahead. Then turn left into the adjoining field, keeping the copse on your right. When you meet another ditch go right and then almost immediately left, to cross a substantial wooden bridge. The area beyond can be rather overgrown, especially with nettles, but you just keep ahead, turning slightly to the right as you follow the stream on your left.

After 100 yards or so you will see a second wooden bridge on your left. Cross both it and the stile beyond. You are now in another grassy field – often grazed by very small ponies. Turn right and go to the end of the field, crossing another stile into a lane. This soon meets a roadway by a Public Footpath sign. Turn left and walk uphill into Upend.

Description continued overleaf

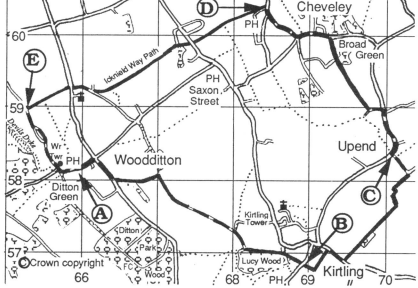

Upend

At the road junction ahead **C**, turn right and follow the road round for a further 500 yards. There are a number of fine thatched houses in the village, but no shop or PH. Follow a Public Footpath sign pointing left down a lane; 200 yards further on there is another sign, this time pointing to the right. You pass through a wooden gate into paddock country!

Your route goes slightly to your right between the paddock fences, with a hedge on your right, and fencing on your left. Cross the first roadway (waymarked), then the second, this time following a grass track between two sets of fences to the right, passing by a brick house. You cross a stile and join a drive. Keep on this to the road, where there is a Public Footpath sign pointing back along your route and a sign for Banstead Manor Stud. You have now walked 5.5 miles.

Turn left and walk along the country lane for 350 yards, beyond the village green. Take the road signposted Cheveley and Moulton to the right. There is a pavement on the right-hand side. This is Coach Lane. As it comes into Cheveley proper the Red Lion pub is directly opposite.

Cheveley

Turn right at the road junction, past the village shop and post office. After 100 yards there is a Public Bridleway sign to the left. Turn onto it, joining the Icknield Way path **D**. As it is shared with horses it is often rather muddy! After 1200 yards cross the road, marked Saxon Street to your left, go over the stile and take the cross-field path ahead. Climb over the stile on the other side of the field, walk through the narrow belt of trees and turn left onto a chalk and grass track. You now have a hedge on your right. Continue along the track until you pass through some Scots pines. The track now passes between two open fields. On the other side you pick up a hedge on your left with two houses beyond and the path soon becomes tarmac.

Woodditton

Keep on the track, turning gently right. When you come to a road junction, with Woodditton Church ahead, turn right. This lane now passes the Church on your left before coming to the junction with the Ditton Green Road. Turn right (Maypole Lane) and then very soon left, following a track marked with a 'Public Footpath' sign. After 650 yards turn left onto a broad stony track which crosses your path **E**.

Go through the white metal gate ahead and, after 50 yards, turn slightly left, off the main drive, keeping a wooden fence on your left. This bridleway takes you round to the E of the remaining Camois Hall buildings – mainly stables. You soon join the main drive again. Keep left, passing a modern bungalow in the field on your right. First pass through a white wooden gate – and then you come into Ditton Green again, passing a large water tower on your left. At the road, turn left – back to your car or the pub!

25 Kirtling – Burrough Green circular

9 miles / 14 kilometres

Start: Kirtling Green **A** [678562]
Transport: Bus – from Newmarket
Maps: Landranger 154; Pathfinder 1005
Refreshments: Kirtling – The Red Lion PH
                Burrough Green – The Bull PH
                Ditton Green – The Three Blackbirds PH

Points of interest:

Aqueduct carrying water from Suffolk to Essex
Burrough Green church and old school (figures over
door)

Kirtling Green

Start from the Woodditton Road along a narrow lane (with wide verges) running SW. Follow the lane for half a mile with pleasant views of Great Widgham Wood and Great Bradley. At the end of the metalled road, cross the bridge over an aqueduct carrying water to the River Stour, and turn right immediately along the bank, ignoring the adjacent gated soft road with a sign 'Private – No Admittance'. Walk downstream past 3 weirs with bridges. At the fourth weir, turn right by a wooden signpost, and cross the river **B** [673552].

Turn half-right across a narrow strip of arable land and walk along the N side of Great Widgham Wood. Pass through a gap at the end of a crossing hedge, and continue by the wood on a good headland for a further 200 yards. The wood boundary on the left then gives way to a ditch and fence, which follow across to the corner of Ten Wood **C** [666555].

Cross a small concrete bridge over the ditch on the left, and continue in the same direction with paddock railings on left and Ten Wood on right. When the fence ends, continue in the same direction along a headland with wood on right, and arable on left. Cross a ditch by a wide earth bridge, and continue on the wide grassy headland. 25 yards beyond the end of the wood, cross back onto the right side of the ditch and continue on a grassy headland for one field to **D** [659562]. Here, cross back over the ditch by a narrow earth bridge, and continue with the old hedge on the right, and newly planted trees and railings on the left.

A fine new wooden bridge is crossed after 200 yards, and the path is followed past Basefield Wood on the right. At the end of the wood is a narrow chicane between the railings (thin people only!), and after a further 35 yards, turn left through another narrow gap in the rails **E** [647569] to walk S downhill between paddock railings. Continue between railings and later, a hedge on left, to cross a bridge with yellow and white metal rails and gain the road at Dullingham Ley over a new stile beside Rising Sun Cottage **F**.

Dullingham Ley

Turn right along the road for 150 yards, passing a telephone box and The Mission Room, then left by a wooden signpost next to a bungalow (house number 24). Cross the bridge over the roadside ditch, and walk S between paddock fences, crossing a metalled farm road. At a T-junction veer left with ditch on right. At the end of the field, duck under a high cross bar, then follow the next fence round the right hand side of a paddock towards an old burial ground with fir trees. Here join a a slightly sunken green lane, which becomes metalled, and leads into Burrough Green, by Walnut Tree Cottages.

Description continued overleaf

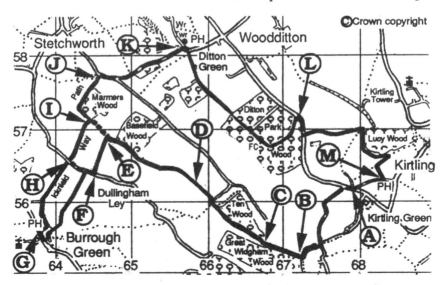

Burrough Green

Turn right along the pavement of the B1061, passing the Post Office on right, and the Old School and Church on the other side of the Green, to reach The Bull PH, **G**. Turn right with pub car park on your left over an area of rough grass. Beyond the car park, turn left in front of a fence, to follow a footpath along the backs of the houses, which passes an old orchard, before striking out as a grass track, following telegraph poles across a field towards a pink cottage. We are now on the line of the Icknield Way LDP, which leads from Ivinghoe Beacon, Buckinghamshire, to Knettishall Heath, Suffolk. Turn half-right to pass in front of the row of cottages along a green lane back to Dullingham Ley **H**.

Cross the road to the footpath immediately opposite. Follow this between hedge and railings, passing behind a cottage garden, crossing a shallow ditch, and making right and left turns to continue in the generally NE direction between paddock fences towards Marmer's Wood **I** [645572]. In front of the wood, turn left for 100 yards, and beyond the wood corner, turn right over a shallow ditch to join a headland along the W side of the wood. Continue to the far end of the wood, where you cross a concrete bridge with handrail, and turn half-left with ditch and hedge on left, going downhill to meet the Stetchworth road at double gates **J**.

Turn right along the verge of this road for three-quarters of a mile to Ditton Green, ignoring the deadend road on the right signposted Stetchworth Ley. In the village, turn right by the huge concrete water tower, then after 75 yards, leave the road down West End (or follow the road left for 200 yards to the Three Blackbirds PH!). West End **K** soon becomes a pleasant wide hedged green lane leading SE for half a mile to the Forestry Commission's Ditton Park Wood. Paths in the wood are not recorded on the Definitive Rights of Way Map, but are well-used by the public. Enter the wood over a low hurdle, and continue along a broad ride ahead, through attractive mixed woodland. Ignore a sandy track turning left and continue SE for a further 600 yards, taking the next left turn along a sometimes damp track to reach the road by a gate at **L** [671572].

Turn right along the road, shortly passing Park Cottage on the left. After a further 200 yards, turn left down a signposted track with ditch on right, leading E to Lucy Wood. 50 yards before reaching the wood, go through a field entrance on the right, and continue on a green track with hedge on left. Turn right at the wood, going S along the field edge, with wood and pheasant pens on the left. At the wood corner, turn left and continue to follow the edge of the wood until stopped by a crossing hedge **M** [683566]. Here, turn right, with hedge and fence on left, and continue for 350 yards, to the hedge-corner. Turn left, still with hedge on left, to reach a lane by a former Methodist Chapel (now a garage). Turn right along the broad green byway between hedges to meet the Woodditton Road. Turn right again to return to the start **A** in 100 yards.

Shorter walks can be taken as follows:

■   Continuing from Basefield wood **E** to Marmer's Wood **I** – 7.5 miles.

■   Turning round at Dullingham Ley, by walking along the road between points **F** and **H** – 8.5 miles.

■   A very short circuit may be made from Burrough Green to Marmer's Wood, Basefield Wood, via Dullingham Ley – points **G, H, I, E, F, G** – 2.5 miles.

26 Burrough Green circular

6 miles / 9.5 kilometres

Start: Burrough Green **A** [638555]
Maps: Landranger 154; Pathfinder 1005
Transport: Bus – from Cambridge or Newmarket
Refreshments: Burrough Green – Bull PH

The walk starts and ends at a side street off the B1061 road
named Walnut Tree Cottages **A**, opposite the green, about 150
yards past the pub in the Great Bradley direction. Go down
Walnut Tree Cottages and take the left spur, leading into a
lane at the end, ignoring a Public Footpath sign just to the
right. Just beyond the last house on the right in the lane there
is an old wooden shed. Turn right just beyond it. Follow a
grassy track to the edge of a field and skirt it, keeping the field
on your left.

Coming into the next open field you can see agricultural
buildings on your right and isolated trees on the field
boundary ahead. Make for the tree on the right, next to a
causeway which crosses the field edge ditch – if the field is
ploughed and/or cropped it may be easier to go round the
edge. Cross the causeway, picking up an earth track which
comes from the right through the farm buildings. Follow this
track which runs E for about 600 yards, before swinging to
the right.

Keep on the track – grassy now – until it comes to a field edge.
Here it meets a very wide grassy track. Turn left and follow the
track along the edge of the wood – Bushy Grove. Keep on the
track as it rounds a corner to the right, and then turns sharp
left into Out Wood **B**.

Follow the track for 100 yards through the wood, emerging on
its S side. Turn left and follow the field edge path with the
wood on your left. Cross a stile at the next fence and keep
along the edge of the wood. Cross another fence by a stile. The
route now veers slightly to the right across the grassy field –
up the slight rise ahead. On the other side cross over a
wooden stile and bridge set in the hedge, then continue
alongside Plunder Wood, with the wood on your left. At the
corner turn diagonally left on the path across the field.

After 400 yards you come to a ditch. If there is no bridge and crossing is a problem there is an old bridge which has definitely seen better days about 200 yards along the ditch on your left! – then retrace your steps back along the other side of the ditch.

The route now continues ahead, diagonally across the field, heading for the edge of the woodland – Great Widgham Wood. Crossing the fast flowing stream here **C** is easy, with a choice of vehicular or pedestrian bridges! Once across turn left along the good grassy track. Keep on this track for about 400 yards, past several bridges – until you see a Public Footpath sign pointing to the left. Cross the bridge and aim for the edge of the wood ahead.

Description continued overleaf

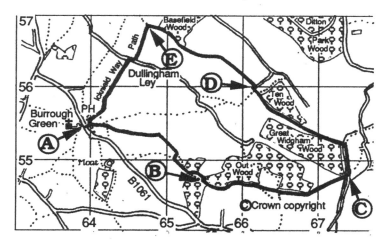

Keep the wood on your left, then a hedge. The path soon swings to the right, meeting up with the corner of Ten Wood. Cross a concrete slab bridge to your left and then turn sharp right. You now have the wood on your right and paddock fencing on your left. Walk alongside the wood to its NW corner **D**. Just past the corner of the field turn into the adjacent field on your right and then turn immediately left – so keeping the same general line, but with a hedge now on your left. After about 200 yards, just beyond a small copse of newly planted trees in the field on your left, turn left through a small gap in the hedge. Turning immediately right you now have the hedge on your right and paddock railings on your left.

The wide track has been planted with trees – a very pleasant walk with paddocks on your left. Cross a stream by means of a substantial foot bridge. You soon pass Basefield Wood on your right. At the end of the wood **E** pass between the paddock railings ahead. After about 70 yards you will see a double set of paddock railings on your left, stretching down towards stable buildings. There is a gap allowing access and the footpath goes between the fencing. A stile gives onto the road at Dullingham Ley.

Turn right and after 200 yards, just past a house, cross a stile by a Public Footpath sign on your left. Go through the paddock railings on the other side of the field and continue on a path between double fences. After about 400 yards this swings slightly to the left, forming a track through a newly planted copse. Through yet more paddock railings – a cross bar has been removed to make this easy – and, once over a footbridge, turn first right, then left and left again to walk round a paddock. This path was officially re-routed in 1991 and does not go straight across the paddock as may be indicated on the Ordnance Survey maps. Now the path swings to the right. It is first a green lane – then more stony – and you are back in Burrough Green.

27 Great Bradley – Kirtling circular

7.5 miles / 12 kilometres

Start: Great Bradley, church **A** [674532]
Maps: Landranger 154; Pathfinder 1005
Refreshments: Kirtling – Red Lion PH

Points of interest:
    Kirtling Tower

Great Bradley

A Take the road to Cowlinge. After half a mile, just past a house on the right, a lane to the left is signposted East Green. Take it and continue past a number of houses in the hamlet. After the last house carry on for a further 400 yards, ignoring two tracks off to the right. You will then come to a Public Bridleway sign pointing along a hedge to the right. Follow this, keeping the hedge on your right. The field is grassy and very easy walking.

A further 600 yards on you should find another Public Bridleway sign, with your direction turning slightly to the left. Keep a hedge on your right, and then a ditch. Soon you cross an earth bridge into a cropped field **B**. Turn right, keeping on the field headland, and follow the field corner round, first right, then left. You can see the path we will be taking signposted about 30 yards away.

On reaching this next Public Bridleway post, cross the ditch on your right by a wooden plank bridge. You are now in a wide green lane which you follow through to Sharp's Green for 500 yards. Here you meet a hard surfaced track – with a Public Byway sign pointing back the way you've come, and a Public Footpath sign pointing your way left. A further 250 yards on you pass Pratts Green Farm on your right and meet a road; turn right.

After 200 yards you come to a road junction by a post box; take the track to your left. First you have trees on your left. Then, after 60 yards, keeping on the same line, you pick up a hedge on your right. The right of way follows this hedge gently round to the right. You soon meet paddock fencing on your left and a substantial hedge on your right. Cross over the stile on your left into a grassy field and turn right, walking alongside the fencing. Cross over a further stile into the next field.

At the next corner, where the fencing turns sharply left, cross over a second stile, out of the paddocks. Here you need to turn first right through a narrow tree belt and then immediately left over a plank bridge. Now go straight ahead, between high hedges in an old lane – if overgrown, go round the field edge on your left. You emerge by a white cottage. Take the cottage drive to the road **C**. By now you have covered about 3 miles.

Kirtling

Turn left, cross the road and climb over a stile by a Public Footpath sign on your right. You are now in another grassy field. Walk along the garden hedge on your left hand side and, at the corner, turn slight left, walking down across the field towards a gap in a hedgerow ahead. Looking to the right you can see Kirtling Tower on the hillside. Once through the hedge walk towards the wooden gate ahead. Pass through the kissing gate alongside and over the wooden bridge. At a junction of several muddy tracks you should turn left.

After 200 yards the track you are on swings left, but keep straight on, taking a footpath now just inside the wood. You pass over a stream just before coming to a clearing. The path now becomes a track again, running just outside the wood. Turn left, and 100 yards further on turn left again, keeping Lucy Wood on your left. There is a good broad grassy headland. At the next corner of the wood turn left once more – yes, you're walking three-quarters of the way round the wood!

The right of way passes SE across the field ahead – if not reinstated, keep to the headland by the wood. After 200 yards, when you come to the end, or corner, of the wood, turn right, with a ditch and hedge now on your left. The headland may be rather poor. After a further 200 yards cross a bridge over the deep ditch on your left. The path now passes between two paddock fences. At the time of writing, this could be a bit tricky – you have to step between three sets of fences and over a shallow ditch before you get to a lane.

Cross straight over the lane, following the Public Footpath signs. You now have a good wide headland path, with a hedge on your right. At the next road **D** turn right. You can see a Public Footpath sign on your left. Follow it down a short green lane. You are now just above the reservoir which feeds the river which you accompany for the next mile and more. First you have to walk round the reservoir, keeping to the field headland, with fencing on your right. Once you meet the river the right of way follows the E, left, bank – but as it is often ploughed and cropped it is common practice to take the easiest route. When you meet a tarmac road, after 600 yards, cross it and keep to the left bank of the river.

Description continued overleaf

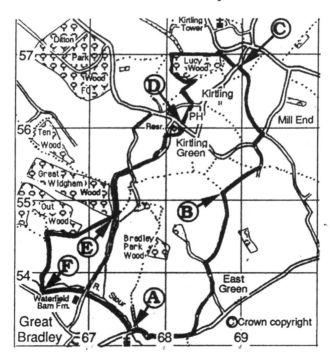

You soon pass Great Widgham Wood on your right. About 50 yards beyond the end of the wood a right of way crosses the river once more **E**. Here you have a choice of route. The simplest option is to keep on the well used track for a further half a mile to Waterfield Barn. This is a right of way, but this is not clear from the current map!

If you want a slightly longer route, shown as a broken line on the map, cross the river just beyond Great Widgham Wood and then diagonally cross a cropped field to your left. Cross the ditch on your left by a new bridge if it has been built – otherwise seek out a very dilapidated wooden plank bridge on your right, nearer Plunder Wood. Continue along the cross-field path in the same direction, to the corner of Plunder Wood, where you should turn right.

At the end of this field and the end of the wood on your right, cross over a new bridge and stile. Turn left and follow the hedge for 150 yards until you come to another new stile and bridge on your left. Cross them and turn right. Follow the headland S, keeping first the hedge, then a ditch, on your right. When you reach a second shallow ditch across your path, cross it and follow the headland S, first to a stile, then a new bridge **F** over the River Stour. Cross it, then turn left into a grassy field.

Continue E, keeping a hedge on your right. In 400 yards easy walking you come to Waterfield Barn Farm, and meet up with the track we were on before turning off at Great Widgham Wood. Cross over a stile on your right, and cross the track. Turn right and then almost immediately left. Follow a signpost pointing along a wide field headland path, with a hedge and ditch on your left now. In about 500 yards the path crosses the ditch on the left. Now follow the headland path, first to the left, then after 20 yards to the right, alongside the main river again. In 300 yards you are back at a Public Footpath sign on the Great Bradley/Cowlinge Road, near the Church.

28 Great Bradley – Longacre Green – Kirtling circular

8 miles / 13 km

Start: Great Bradley, Water Lane **A** [667533]
Maps: Landranger 154; Pathfinder 1005
Transport: Bus – Haverhill to Newmarket via Great
                        Bradley
Refreshments: Kirtling – PH
                        Great Bradley – **none**

Points of interest:
Great Bradley church – Tudor brick porch with fine
  decorated Norman doorway, 12th century nave
The 'Grundle' on the walk **G** [676549] is a sunken
  passage, formed naturally by running water which,
  having carved its way through boulder clay, then sinks
  into the permeable strata beneath, forming a generally
  dry lane
Lucy Wood – ancient, with many interesting plants

From Water Lane, Great Bradley **A** walk N down the lane
towards the ford **B** [669538]. In front of the ford, turn right
opposite a barn, along a signposted wide grassy footpath with
hedge on left. At the end of the field, pass to the left of some
pine trees, turn left by a ditch, then right after 50 yards to
continue alongside the River Stour. Follow this SE to the road
at **C** – Great Bradley Church lies 100 yards to the right. Turn
left over the bridge, and, after a few yards, left again at the
signpost indicating the footpath running N up a concrete farm
road. Follow this, turning half-right at the end of the first field,
uphill to Bradley Park Wood. At the wood, pass through the
hedge on the left **D** [677543] to continue with the wood on the
right. Beyond the wood, continue in the same direction on a
grassy headland path, with ditch and hedge on right.

Where the headland ends at a crossing hedge **E** [679547], a
waymark indicates a turning half-left along the headland for
20 yards, then across a ditch on a sleeper bridge. Walk
approximately N across the arable field, towards an island of
scrub in the middle of the field, which marks the site of a
former farmstead, Horse Pasture Farm. Continue forward
beyond this, to the field boundary, where a second waymark
indicates an earth bridge over a ditch **F** [679548].

Cross the bridge, and turn left with ditch on left and follow the field edge until a wood is reached. Go forward in the same direction, (approximately W) on a cleared track through the wood, to reach a wooden 'Public Footpath' signpost **G**. To continue the walk, turn right onto an open wide grassy byway, flanked by ditches. It is worthwhile making a detour to the left to look at the Grundle – see 'Points of interest' above.

Returning to the byway, follow the track NW past a small copse and round right and left bends, passing some sheds (all that remains of Longacre Green Farm) to reach a concrete bridge over the conduit feeding the River Stour **H** [675554]. Cross the bridge, and turn immediately right along the raised bank with water on the right – although some maps show the right of way along the other bank of the conduit, there is no path. Houses at Kirtling Green can be seen ahead.

After nearly half a mile, by a small valve house on the bank, cross the conduit on a railed bridge, and take the diverted right of way around the front of a grassy mound, and continue around the field edge, shortly joining the grass strip in front of a wooden fence, which surrounds the underground reservoir. The path emerges up a short track onto the road at Kirtling Green **I** [681561]. Turn right here, then left at a road junction, for the pub!

Opposite the former school **J** take a signposted path over a stile into a meadow with fine lime trees. Continue NW, half-left, through a gap in the hedge on the other side of the field, into a second meadow, where head for a kissing-gate under chestnut trees in the far corner.

Go through the kissing-gate, over a footbridge, and immediately turn left along a thistly bridleway inside the N edge of Lucy Wood. Keep close to the edge of the wood, and where a broad ride comes in from the right, continue ahead on an earth track with the wood and later a tall hedge on the left. 50 yards beyond the edge of the wood, turn left through a gap in the hedge, and double back towards the wood, on a broad grassy track. Follow the edge of the wood round to right, turning left at the next corner, and following a reinstated (corner-cutting) path until a crossing ditch and hedge are reached behind some paddocks **K** [683566].

Here turn right along the narrow headland, with ditch and hedge on left, and follow it round to the left, to emerge in a yard by a disused Primitive Methodist Chapel, now used as a storage shed. Turn right along the grassy byway between hedges, to emerge onto the Woodditton Road near **I**. Turn right along the road, left after 100 yards down a narrow tarmac lane, with No Through Road sign **L**.

Walk down the lane to meet the conduit again at point **H**. Cross the bridge, and this time, turn right along the bank (ignore the 'Private' sign on a gate, which refers to the adjacent farm track). Walk downstream, passing Great Widgham Wood. A shallow concrete ford, usually dry, can be avoided if necessary by crossing the conduit on a concrete bridge, continuing along the field edge, and recrossing by another bridge 200 yards downstream. About 300 yards beyond this point, the conduit swings left, but the main track crosses it by a bridge, and continues ahead to the ford and footbridge over the River Stour at point **B**. Return up the lane to point **A**, and waiting car.

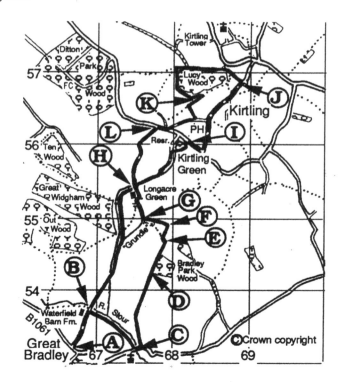

29 Ely – Newmarket linear

16 miles / 26 km

Start: Ely Rail Station **A** [543794]
Finish: Newmarket Rail Station **F** [644627]
Maps: Landranger 143, 156; Pathfinder 961, 982, 983
Transport :   Rail & Bus – Ely and Newmarket are served
                    from Cambridge and Bury St. Edmunds
Refreshments: Upware – Five Miles from Anywhere PH
                    Reach – The King's PH
                    Newmarket – PH and teashops

Points of interest:
        Reach port – information board on site
        Devils Dyke
        Newmarket Racecourse
        Commissioners Pit nature reserve

Turn right onto the road at the end of the station approach, cross the river, and 100 yards beyond turn right over a stile to join the river floodbank. The next few miles follow pleasantly along the river until, after crossing a stile, the ground beneath your feet turns to cultivated grass and the path soon turns away from the river. After 400 yards, at a path junction, turn right onto a track and over a bridge, leading S to the busy A1123 **B**. Cross over and continue along the track opposite. This widens to a splendid green lane, passing the Commissioners Pit nature reserve on your right.

The lane gives onto an arable field where you should turn right and then shortly left, along a track at the edge. At the end of the field continue ahead over a stile, through a small field, keeping alongside a hedge on your right. Crossing the stile ahead, you emerge by the aptly named PH 'Five Miles from Anywhere', a good lunchtime stopping place.

Upware

The walk continues past the pub along an embankment, the path curving left to reach a road. You have now walked about 7 miles.

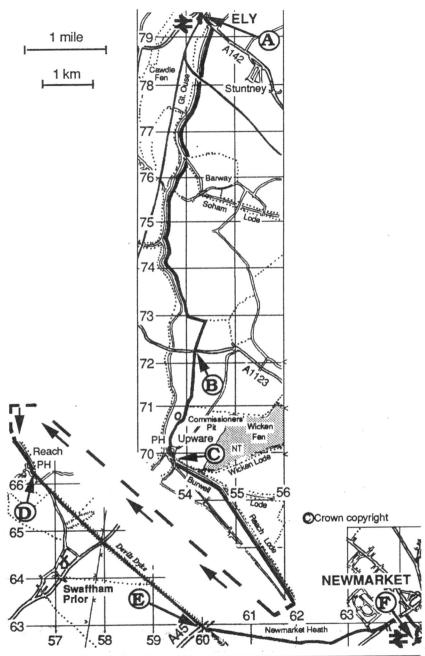

1 mile

1 km

ELY

Ⓐ

A142

Cawdle Fen

Stuntney

Gt. Ouse

Barway

Soham Lode

A1123

Ⓑ

Commissioners' Pit

Wicken Fen

PH

Upware

Ⓒ

NT

Wicken Lode

Burwell

Reach

PH

Ⓓ

Reach Lode

Soham Lode

© Crown copyright

Swaffham Prior

Devils Dyke

Ⓔ

Newmarket Heath

NEWMARKET

Ⓕ

Turn right at the road and continue, to cross a bridge by a lock **C**. Turn left onto the stream bank, with Reach Lode on your left. The embankment path takes you in a straight line almost all the way to Reach. Just before reaching the first houses, cross a stile and 70 yards later turn left over a concrete footbridge, turning immediately right and continuing into the village.

Reach D

It seems hard to believe that Reach was once a busy port, particularly between the 14th and 18th centuries. Trade finally died out in the 1930s, but Reach Lode, believed to have been built by the Romans, remains navigable. Village fairs have taken place in Reach since 1201. The King's PH, on the E side of the village green, is another recommended watering hole. Reach is just over 10 miles from your start.

At the S end of the green an impressive hedge marks the beginning of the Devils Dyke. A path can be followed inside the hedge, and takes you much of the rest of the way to Newmarket. Information boards are placed at intervals to give a brief history of the Dyke.

Cross the A45 dual carriageway **E** by a pedestrian bridge; after crossing a stile, leave the Dyke and follow a route over the grassland to its left. This takes you over the racecourse first towards and then behind the main grandstand; please note that the racecourse is not a right-of-way, although generally used when racing is not taking place. Alternatively, continue along the right-of-way along the top of the Dyke as far as the Newmarket/Cambridge road, turning left along the grassy verge into Newmarket.

The far end of the course brings you close to the town of Newmarket, which houses the National Horse Racing Museum. The railway station is reached by turning right off the main street before reaching the Museum, and there are pubs and tea shops in the town to provide yet another refreshment stop.

30 Newmarket – Haverhill linear

17 miles / 27 km

Start:	Newmarket Rail Station **A** [643627]
Finish:	Haverhill Bus Station **M** [671455]
Maps:	Landranger 154; Pathfinder 983, 1005, 1028
Transport:	Rail & Bus – from Cambridge to Newmarket Bus – from Haverhill to Cambridge
Refreshments:	Wood Ditton – Three Blackbirds PH Little Thurlow – The Cock PH Great Wratting – PH Haverhill – cafes, PHs

Newmarket

Turn left out of the station **A**, taking Paddock Lane to the end. Turn right, then left at the next road junction, and continue along the grass verge of the road for just over a mile. 500 yards past the driveway to Crockfords Farm, turn left on to a signed public bridleway **B**. The Devils Dyke can be seen in the distance running roughly parallel off to the right.

Continue to Dane Bottom where the Icknield Way long distance path crosses, carry on round Camois Hall, after which a gentle climb brings you out at a water tower at Ditton Green **C**. Take the road ahead for 50 yards, when it turns left go straight on along West End (or stay on the main road for the 1642-vintage Three Blackbirds PH about 200 yards away – meals served every day).

After the last house, West End becomes a grass track leading to Ditton Park Wood, where you may be lucky enough to see deer. This is managed by the Forestry Commission; the tracks and rides may be used as permissive paths, although not marked specially on maps. A broad track leads SE through the wood; after 600 yards turn left at the staggered junction of tracks and continue for a further 400 yards to a lane **D**.

Turn right onto the lane, round a right hand bend, then take the signed footpath on the left, with a ditch on the right, which leads to Lucy Wood. Where the track turns sharp left by the wood, go straight ahead along a bridleway following the edge of the wood. At the end, go over a footbridge to the right, through a kissing gate, half left to a gap in the hedge, then slightly right, heading for an old school building. Emerge via a stile onto a lane **E**. This is Kirtling.

Kirtling

Turn left, then right after the old school, up a track and into a sunken path between hedges (if overgrown, use the field edge on the right). Cross a plank bridge ahead, turn right and step over a waymarked stile into a paddock. Turn left and follow round the field, with paddock fencing on your left. Cross a second stile into the next field. After some distance, the fence bears right away from the hedge, and you cross a stile and bear left with the hedge to emerge on a track leading to a lane at Mill End. Turn right on the lane, and at the next bend, turn left at Pratts Green Farm. At the end of the lane, turn right along a signed byway and along a green lane to a plank bridge and T junction by a signpost. Turn left here, right at field corner, left through gap in 20 yards, to follow a hedge on the left. The path inclines gently and continues to meet a metalled track. Turn left and follow the track to a road junction at East Green **F**.

Turn right, and left in 20 yards along a signed footpath with a hedge on the left. At the field corner go through a gap on the left. Your waymarked route should follow the same line – almost due S, but may be obstructed by crops, involving a detour right, then left and left again round the field edge. Cross this field, and then the next, to meet a track with a hedge on the right and follow it to a lane. Turn right down the lane into Little Bradley, past the tiny church, a telephone box, and a bridge over a river **G**. Turn left just after the bridge onto a path leading between fields (or follow the well-walked river bank) until you pass along the left of a small cemetery adjoining Little Thurlow Church **H**.

Description continued on page 98

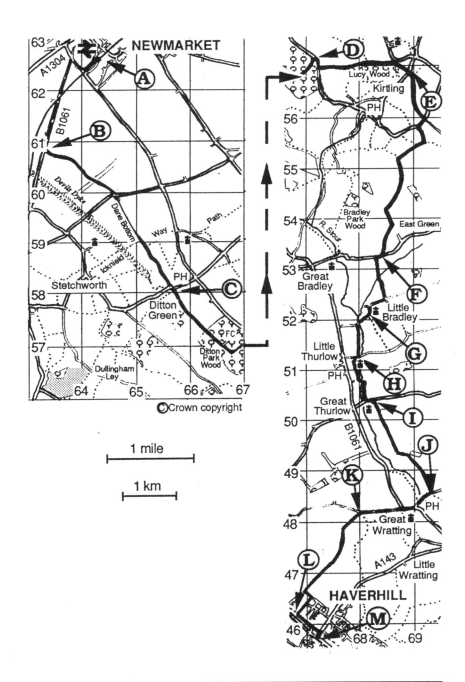

NEWMARKET

1 mile

1 km

©Crown copyright

Little Thurlow

Turn right on the lane, then left just past the church, and immediately diagonally right on a path between fences. Cross a footbridge, and then cross a field diagonally left to a stile in the hedgerow. Cross the next field, climbing another stile into a small wood. The path through the wood swings first left, then right to a fence and stile. Climb over this, turning left into a lane. If you want refreshment, turn right down the lane to the main Little Thurlow – Great Thurlow road and The Cock PH; refreshed,. retrace your steps back up the lane.Follow the lane to a bridge over the river – cross it and immediately turn right. Follow this path S to reach another small cemetery and a lane at Great Thurlow **I**.

Turn left, pass the church and turn right at Hall Farm onto a footpath between farm buildings. The concrete path passes some attractive parkland before becoming an earth track. At the end, go into the next field, immediately turn right over a bridge in the hedge, then left to follow the hedge. Near the end of this field, cross a gate, turn right and follow a field edge with a new hedge on your left. The path may be obstructed with crops, but just past a small copse of trees on your left you should pick up a track, where you turn right and follow a lane to Great Wratting **J**.

Great Wratting

Turn right, join the B1061, continue past the church, and take a lane on the left signposted to Withersfield. Past some attractive cottages turn left up Moor Pasture Way **K**, once on a coaching route between Haverhill and Newmarket. A concrete track climbs to command extensive views near a water tower. A rough track continues ahead with the outskirts of Haverhill visible, then continues as a path between hedges. Continue along the field edge path, and pass between wooden fences at the field corner.

Turn left to pass between houses. At a crossing tarmac path, turn right and continue to the line of the old Cambridge/Haverhill railway line, marked by an old brick bridge **L**. As you approach the bridge, fork slightly to the right, then turn left to join the railway line. Follow this all the way to a main road, turn right onto the road and turn left at the next junction. Keep to the right hand side of this road, the main traffic bypass for the town centre; the bus station **M** is soon reached on the right, almost opposite the Sports Centre.